Faith, Hope… and a Miracle in Africa

J.C. Mustarde

Faith, Hope… and a Miracle in Africa

How a group of volunteer surgeons brought a desperately needed
branch of surgery to a poverty stricken third-world country

Jack Mustardé

First Published in 2005 by
Serendipity
First floor
37/39 Victoria Road
Darlington

British Library Cataloguing-in-Publication data

A catalogue record for this book is available from the British Library

ISBN 1-84394-157-0

Printed and bound by The Alden Press

FOREWORD

'Do not be afraid for the Lord will go before you. He will not fail or forsake you.'

(Deut. 31:8)

After a full and distinguished career in medicine, Mr Jack Mustardé had earned a restful retirement. At the age of 77 Jack had every right to head for the golf course or riverside where he could have enjoyed the fruit of his labour and a little peace and quiet. Not for one minute did Jack succumb to temptation. Instead, he had the courage to begin a project in Ghana and the determination to finish it. Along the way he has inspired so many to share in his dream: as Jack's minister, it is my privilege to commend to you the story of how Jack's House came to be built. Not only has Jack's faith inspired his own congregation in Alloway, I feel certain this story will also inspire you.

The truth is, for all our good work, regardless of age... it is never too late to begin.

Reverend Neil McNaught
Alloway Parish Church, Ayr

£16,000 donated by church

This book is dedicated to my beloved wife, with grateful thanks for all her patience

ACKNOWLEDGEMENTS

Martyn Webster FRCS

Arthur Morris FRCS

Prof. Edward Yeboah (Professor of Surgery, Ghana University)

Mr Ronald Shannon (my most helpful typist and adviser)

CHAPTER 1

It was hot, incredibly hot, with an intensity that made the still air feel almost solid as I breathed it, and I could feel the perspiration trickling steadily down my back – and dripping embarrassingly off my nose. Even the face of the patient sitting opposite us glistened with perspiration, and she was black and used to the heat. For this was Ghana, right on the Equator, and it was mid-afternoon, when no one in his right mind, white or black, would be working, unless with the benefit of air-conditioning. But the air conditioning units fixed to the windows on either side of the room were not working, and the open door and windows did nothing to reduce the intensity of the heat.

There were four of us gathered round the female Ghanaian patient: two Argentine plastic surgeons with their accompanying paediatrician, and myself – a seventy-four-year-old retired Scottish plastic surgeon. We were holding a clinic in a room in the rundown wooden building in the old 35th Military Hospital (later largely rebuilt) in Accra, the capital of Ghana. It was January 1992 in one of the hottest periods of the year – or rather the most humid – and the stifling heat never changed, at least as far as non-residential white folk like us were concerned.

The patient, a thirty-year-old Ghanaian woman, had been badly burned about the face and chest four years ago, and the resulting scarring had contracted to such an extent that her lower lip was fixed to her chest, with saliva constantly dripping down over her clothing. I had seldom seen anything like it since I had been a surgeon in the army in World War II, and I knew it would involve a great deal of complicated surgery to free her mouth and lower jaw from the chest and cover the raw area that would result with extensive skin grafts from her thighs.

It was the third Monday in January 1992 and we had arrived in Ghana over the weekend; with Alberto Ferriols, the team leader, and the rest of the Argentines coming in from Delhi on Saturday – whilst I arrived on Sunday evening from UK – at the start of a three-week visit as a volunteer Plastic Surgery team under the auspices of Rotary International (although I was no longer a Rotarian myself).

At 7.30 that morning, in the deceptive cool of the early part of the day, we had been brought in a minibus to the Hospital, more or less in the centre of Accra, the capital of Ghana, and had been driven round to the out-patient department where we would be able to examine the prospective patients and decide on any surgery we could carry out to help them. Swinging round the corner of the building we had been astounded to find a queue, nearly 100 yards long, of families, mostly squatting on the ground, as is the African custom, eating their breakfast. It turned out that the news of our impending arrival had been broadcast on TV and published in the papers some weeks ago, and families had travelled two, and even three, days bringing their afflicted family members in the hope that we could help them.

We were going to be operating on each of four days in Accra, then go up to Kumasi, the capital of the Ashanti Kingdom, for a week, and come back down again to Accra for a final five days operating. From the beginning, however, it had been patently obvious that we would only be able to cope with a fraction of the people who had come to see us, but we had to make a start examining them in order to plan out what we would be able to deal with.

As we began the rather difficult task of deciding who we would and who we would not operate on, we were surprised to find that quite a high proportion of the patients suffered from the effects of burning accidents, and that most of them were children. It seemed that in the rural areas, where most of them lived in grass-roofed huts, the mother would cook the meals on a Primus stove just outside the doorway, often with the children crowded into the hut, and a spark or flare-up of the stove could result in the children being trapped in the burning hut. If they did survive, it was often with severe scarring of the face and limbs, reducing them to cripples unable to cope with their share of the work of the family, and only able to beg in the street – if even that.

There were also many children with cleft lip and palate, and a few adults with untreated lip and palate problems. There were four patients with cancrum oris, a tropical disease in which bacteria combine to produce deep destruction of tissue around the mouth and the bone of the upper jaw, and we found ourselves encountering for the first time a new disease sweeping parts of Africa and other tropical areas, Buruli ulcer, named from the African town it had first been reported on five years earlier. We saw three cases of the disease, presenting as very large deep ulcers on different parts of the body, but until then no cure had been found for it and the ulcers tended to recur despite being apparently totally cut out and the area skin grafted – the only procedure open to us.

Although we had hoped to see eight to nine, or even more, patients an hour, the increasing heat, and the magnitude of the problems we were encountering, slowed us up considerably, and by one o'clock we had to call a halt for a brief lunch break.

One thing which had become very obvious to us was that if there had been surgeons trained to deal with the type of problems we had been examining, a large number of them would never have reached the stage we had seen. It also made us realize that, apart from the length of time that the surgery of the more complicated cases would involve, it would be wrong to leave behind possible nursing or surgical problems to the care of staff inexperienced in coping with the kind of difficulties to which the type of surgery we would be carrying out may at times give rise.

Although ruthless selection was the only sensible way to handle this situation it was a heartbreaking decision to make when one knew one could do *something* for almost all of these unfortunate people, and because of the numbers, we had to pass on telling those we decided we could not operate on to the attending nursing staff, who could explain our decision to them in their own tongue. The patient with gross contractures of the burn scarring of her neck – a challenge few repair surgeons would have passed up – had sadly to be turned away.

In the end we were able to draw up lists for the four days we would operate in this particular week, and additional lists of those we would operate on in the week after we came back from our visit to Kumasi.

`The Ghana Story' had its beginnings almost two months before, in the latter part of November 1991, when I was the Guest Speaker at the Annual Conference of the Argentine Plastic Surgery Society in Buenos Aires. It was attended by plastic surgeons from many Latin American countries, surgeons I knew well, and I found the experience, albeit in a country with whom we had been at war not so long ago, very stimulating and enjoyable.

Prior to the Conference itself I spent a day as the guest of the Honorary Conference President, who owned an enormous ranch – one sixth the size of Wales, I was told – in the rolling plains of the Pampas. He bred horses, and told me the Duke of Edinburgh had visited him some years before.

The lunch, which was around mid-afternoon, was al fresco under an overhead trelliswork covered in grape vines. The main course was roast pork, and for several hours the delicious aroma of the whole pig turning on a spit over a fire had accompanied the liberal quenching of our thirst with the best champagne.

My host said he understood I enjoyed hunting, and told me he had some of the best hunting in the country. We were going to go out once it was dark, and he was sure I would enjoy it.

As the light began to fade I recollected occasions when, mostly in Africa, I had gone out at night in an open truck with a hunter, armed with a high-powered rifle and with a spot-light clamped on my head, to shoot big game – rather unsuccessfully I have to say. But as we got into the back of my host's Mercedes saloon I was handed a 12-bore shotgun and cartridges such as one would use to shoot pheasants in Scotland...

Driving along fairly slowly through the tall Pampas grass the bright beam of the headlights picked up the occasional hare darting about, or running quickly off into the dark. To my astonishment I was told to hang out of the window and take a shot at them: I fired off about a dozen cartridges, and more by good luck than by good shooting I actually bagged two, whereupon I was hailed as a hero and we headed back to the hacienda to celebrate my achievement.

I was toasted as a Great Hunter, and was informed that I was the first Englander to hit anything...

The Conference itself was very stimulating and I met many old friends whom I had not seen for some time. During the coffee break on the second last day a young man, not known to me, came up to me and asked if he could have a word with me. It turned out that he was about to lead a plastic surgery team to India for two weeks and was then going on to Ghana, in West Africa, for three weeks, in January 1992, and wondered if I would be prepared to join them as adviser to the team.

I had been to India several times, lecturing and demonstrating operations, and I was always pestered by prospective patients, or their relatives, coming to my hotel and wanting me to carry out a cosmetic operation while I was India – at local prices. But I had a never-fail formula for this, and would say that I would be happy to carry out an operation, but for safety's sake I would prefer to do the surgery with the assistance of my own team in Scotland, and I would then hand them my card. I never saw any of them again. Nevertheless, the whole performance was time-consuming, and one couldn't be rude to these callers who, after all, were only looking for what they regarded as the best for their wife or their daughter.

He seemed a rather pleasant young man and I suggested we sit down and he could tell me more about the visit to Ghana he was planning – with one week in Accra, the capital, a week in Kumasi, and a final week back in Accra. As we looked around to find a quiet corner where we could talk uninterruptedly my mind was mulling over what I knew about Ghana. At one time or another over the past fifty years I had been in many different countries in Africa (a few admittedly only briefly as stop-overs), including Nigeria, almost neighbour to Ghana, but I had never been to the latter – the one-time Gold Coast, `The White Man's Grave': a country with an interesting history.

`We know you are retired, Sir,' he began, `but you would not have to do any operating. We would be honoured if you would act as our adviser, and perhaps tell us something of the techniques you have written about in your books.'

I was beginning to warm to this enthusiastic and, it seemed, well-read young fellow, Alberto Ferriols, and when he told me I would be a guest of Rotary International, all expenses paid, I told him that, although it was only some weeks away, I would be pleased to join his team.

When, in late January the following year, I arrived in Ghana, Ferriols met me at the Kotoka Airport, on the outskirts of Accra, and escorted me to where I would be staying. I was more than a little surprised when instead of stopping at one of the better class hotels we drove up to a private house in a row of identical private houses. No one had told me that Rotary International does not put its guests up in posh hotels – or any hotels for that matter – but you are hosted by a local Rotarian in his own home.

I was staying with Rex Owuso-Anso and his family: Rex, a UK-trained lawyer, was the Clerk to the Ghana Parliament, and a High Civil Servant. He lived in a High Civil Servant's house, in a row of High Civil Servants' houses, with no air-conditioning and no shower (one stood in the bath and poured a bucket of water over oneself), but the house was spotless and very comfortable, and he and his beautiful wife Dita, from Assam, were the nicest people one could ever hope to meet. The two separate weeks I was the house guest of the Owuso-Ansos and their young family – to whom I was Uncle Jack – were two of the best times I ever spent in someone else's home.

Rex was the eldest son of a Chief in the northern part of Ghana, and it was part of his tribal duty to offer hospitality to any of his tribe who visited Accra; so the house, with the children in it, was full of `Aunties and Uncles' living in every possible room, and in the various outhouses Rex had put up in the garden, and yet they gave me a large double room with a ceiling fan. I think it was their own room.

It was a little disconcerting to learn later that Ferriols was a guest of Nana (Chief) Asafo-Boatye, the Rotary District Governor and a very successful architect, who had a magnificent air-conditioned house, with a swimming pool, on the outskirts of the city (no matter that the electricity failed to work from time to time) and that the others in the team were hosted by reasonably well-off business men – with swimming pools. Of course, my accommodation had been fixed up at the last moment, and it was extremely good of Rex and Dita to make all the changes in their lifestyle at such short notice: and in any case, when we went up to Kumasi the following week, the boot was well and truly on the other foot.

Although this week and the week after we came back from Kumasi were the only occasions when I stayed with Rex and Dita, we became good friends over the years and I used to drop in for a chat and a cup of coffee whenever I passed the florist shop that Dita ran just off the Ringway, the main road that encircled the heart of Accra.

On one occasion, knowing how much I enjoyed swimming, they took me out to a Country Club of which they were members, and I was intrigued to read the notice beside the swimming pool, on which, at the finish of the usual admonitions about showering before going into the pool etc. it said, 'We do not pee in your bath water: please do not pee in our pool.'

The 35th Military Hospital, built, as many older structures in Accra were, at a time when Ghana was still a British colony, and the place where we were going to be operating, has today a magnificent new multiple operating-theatre suite, fully equipped and run as efficiently as any comparable civilian set-up in any country, but the original theatre block where we operated during our visit was part of the original structure, and was a long way short of that.

Whilst the conditions were scarcely ideal in the Military Hospital, it turned out that the Civilian Hospital at Korle Bu on the west side of the city, also largely built by the British, was awaiting a total reconstruction of the original multi-storey operating-theatre block, and only three theatres were available out of eight, with some surgeons being restricted to a half-day session most weeks. It seemed that the Rotary District Governor had friends in the Military Hospital, where there was no shortage of operating facilities, and had arranged for the Rotary team to have the use of an operating theatre each day it might be required. And whilst these time-expired operating theatres were lacking in much of the sophistication of modern day operating facilities, I was daily intrigued at the antics of a gecko lizard running along the walls apparently watching me scrubbing for surgery.

Although the arrangement had been that I did not have to carry out any surgery – simply give advice – the first patient on Alberto's list had a penile deformity for which I had devised and published an operation, and Alberto persuaded me to carry out the operation while he assisted me, and learned something. He would be honoured to assist me, he said, and I suppose at my age I felt flattered. In any case, especially with some of the more unusual and complex procedures, I was really quite happy to be tackling the surgery myself and not gnawing my lips watching the less experienced, if enthusiastic, young man coping with what for him would often have been quite new situations: and anyhow, I could get the surgery done in a much shorter time than if he was struggling with an unfamiliar problem. So we ended up with Alberto assisting me, both in Accra and in Kumasi during our visit there.

The work proceeded relatively smoothly once the nursing staff was familiar with the type of reparatory surgery we were carrying out, but as the days went by our earlier observation that if there had been surgeons trained in reparative surgery, and especially in the management of severe burns, most of the patients we were seeing would not have needed the specialised help we could give them at all, was confirmed. But we could see no solution to the problem.

It was equally clear to us that, in a country of sixteen million people, where there were so many deformed and disfigured, coming out as we had done for a matter of two or three weeks was like scratching a mountain with a pin for all the good we were doing.

By Friday evening we were all very glad of the weekend break and went to a small, but very attractive French restaurant that had been recommended to us: something we had been unable to do during the week. With a very early start for Kumasi on the Saturday morning, however, we had regretfully to cut short what could have developed into a very pleasant evening.

We finally got off for Kumasi about 7 a.m. and were really looking forward to a change from the sprawling capital city, with its interminable traffic jams. The journey, however, turned out to be one of the roughest rides I have ever experienced, with long stretches of partially repaired road – and some areas with virtually no road surface at all. If we opened the windows to let a breeze in, we were infested with large black biting flies, and if we closed them we nearly suffocated with the heat.

In the early stages the road ran through savannah country with seemingly endless vistas of coarse grass dotted here and there with shrubs or small trees, and without any sign of life except for the occasional few skinny cows herded by small skinny boys; every now and again we would pass a solitary baobab tree – the upside down tree – with the trunk widening from the ground up twenty or thirty feet, where the horizontal ring of branches spreading out sideways looked remarkably like roots. The comparison with parts of South Africa was very marked, and I kept feeling that we might see an antelope now and again, but this was Ghana, where the game had long ago been driven up into the northern part. (Strictly speaking, this is not quite correct, as I was later to discover, as there was a solitary colony of chimpanzees living more or less completely wild, though protected, in a forested area about thirty miles north of Accra – the only wild game in the south, apart from a few species living in a special enclosed park further over towards the west.)

Once we reached the foothills and began gradually climbing we moved out of the savannah country, and the land, apart from low rocky ridges here and there, was largely wooded with a mixture of smaller trees, with the occasional magnificent cotton-wood tree towering high above the rest of the forest and shedding its silky filaments like snow over the nearby vegetation.

The original heavily-wooded African jungle had long ago disappeared over almost all of Ghana – a victim of the world-wide demand for African hardwood – but a few small sections of it had, for one reason or another, survived as protected areas, and at one point we passed through one of these, with the branches of the huge trees spread out a hundred and fifty feet or more above the ground, and forming a continuous canopy which the sun rarely penetrated.

One of the great advantages the town of Kumasi has over Accra is that it lies at over seven hundred feet above sea level, with a corresponding welcome drop in the air temperature, and for the last hour we had been aware of the much needed cooler air – and the absence of the biting flies when we opened the windows. Although the distance between the two towns was less than a hundred miles as the crow flies, the 130 mile roadway was so bad that it took, with a midday break for a snack lunch, some seven hours to make the journey, and we were extremely relieved when the outlying factories and other buildings let us know we were at last approaching Kumasi.

The plan was that we would go direct to our lodgings, and see patients on the Sunday morning in the Komfo Anotye Teaching Hospital (KATE) which was associated with the Technical and Scientific University College. Thereafter we would operate every day from Monday through to Friday afternoon, and return to Accra on Saturday morning.

As we entered the town itself we were struck by the number of trees everywhere – more even than in Accra – and there were many more varieties, with the red-blossomed flamboyant trees predominating. We were also struck by the fact that, apart from its centre, the town is spread out over a number of moderate-sized hills, which makes the place look like a large undulating garden in many areas, until the busy heart of the town is reached.

We drove direct to where I was going to be staying at the house of the Manager of the Shell Company and his wife, where I was made most welcome, and where, for the week I was there, I was extremely comfortable – despite there being no swimming pool.

Before the rest of the team moved off, however, my host explained that the area of Kumasi where the others were being housed – in the Shell Company dormitories – was in a quarter where the water supply had broken down some time ago, and accordingly they could come over to his house for a shower when they felt like it; but he recommended that they should fill up the four-gallon water containers they would find in their rooms when they came over to shower, and that would save them having to make so many trips across the town. I could scarcely contain my amusement at this change in our fortunes – which made up entirely for the lodging arrangements in Accra.

While none of us on this occasion had swimming pools at our doorstep, the men in the team did in fact make an outing to the public open-air swimming pool. It was quite an experience, with the pool packed with so many laughing and shouting youngsters, throwing water over each other and larking about, which made it totally impossible to swim even a couple of strokes. The thing that impressed all of us was the fact that, with our group of four white people floundering about in this sprawling mass of black humanity, no one seemed to take the slightest notice that we were not black like everyone else, and I couldn't help thinking how different it would have been if the colour situation had been reversed.

Situated in the centre of the town, the Komfo Anoyte Hospital, much smaller than the hospital at Korle Bu in Accra, was also built by the British, and perhaps because of the more moderate climate, was in much better condition than the Military Hospital in Accra.

Once again there was the problem of there being no trained plastic surgeons, but the situation was not quite the same as in the Military Hospital and we soon became aware that several of the surgeons, faced with problems of repair and with no plastic surgeon available, had taught themselves some basic forms of repair surgery, including skin grafting and the use of fairly straightforward skin flaps. The oral surgeons had even closed moderate degrees of cleft lip and palate, and they were looking forward very much to our visit – with several intriguing cases to put before us.

Professor Hiadzi, the Head of Surgery, was most enthusiastic about our visit and earnestly asked us not to forget Kumasi if we ever came back to Ghana. He even voiced the hope that some sort of Plastic Surgery Unit might be started up in Accra, with visits to Kumasi.

The surgical problems in Kumasi were on the whole very similar to those in Accra, although there were many more patients suffering from Buruli ulcers, to which this Midland area was particularly prone, but the operating theatres were more modern and reasonably well equipped – and things moved a little faster.

One curious anomaly was that, despite the obvious shortage of operating theatre accommodation, the end theatre in the block of four was used solely as a plaster room for putting on and taking off plaster of Paris splints, mostly on patients with fractures. It appeared that the problem was that they did not have a fourth anaesthetic machine, and no air-conditioning units for that theatre. As we were very soon to learn, additional equipment was low down on the list of hospital requirements all over the country because of the national burden of compulsory repayment of the interest on Ghana's debt to the International Monitory Fund – which is ourselves in UK, amongst others – and which was crippling the country, in common with every country in West Africa.

With the surgical staff familiar with basic reparative procedures, we felt we could tackle more complex conditions, but even so there were still quite a number of disappointed individuals whose surgery we considered too complex for us to leave as potential problems if complications should arise. There was much pleading with us to come back again, which we found embarrassing as we knew this would not happen.

One special pleasure associated with our visit was the team, and wives, being invited to an Audience with the Asantahene – the Ashanti King, Utumfo III, whose grandmother in 1901 was, we understood, one of the leaders of the Ashanti Nation in their third war against the British, which again they lost. I am certain Hiadzi had something to do with this honour, as he was a close friend of the King.

The Audience took place in the still-existing splendour of the Royal Palace, which was spread over quite a large part of the walled Palace grounds, with peacocks strutting about and the males displaying their gorgeously coloured tails to impress the apparently unimpressed females.

The King was most interested in what we were doing in Ghana and begged us to include his people if we should visit Ghana again. As a special privilege we were permitted to have photographs taken of our party ranged on either side of the King, seated on his throne. Unfortunately there was a large mirror as a background directly behind the King and the camera flash reflected back, closing down the camera shutters, with the result that whilst our white faces and shirts came out quite well the black face of the King in his dark cloak was practically invisible.

The surgical work went smoothly, with Ferriols still assisting me and letting me get on with the surgery as I thought fit; and with the help of the Ghanaian surgeons and nurses we got through the week's work with no great problems. Nevertheless it was a relief when, on Friday, the last suture was inserted and the last bandage applied, and after making a last thorough check on the various patients we had operated on, and dealing with one or two matters that had arisen, our hosts then took us out for a very enjoyable out-of-doors supper.

Next morning we were due to leave for Accra, and had planned an early start, but by common consent it was agreed that the effects of the splendid evening we had had really made an early start impractical, and we left around 10 o'clock on the Saturday morning – not relishing the thought of a repeat of the journey coming up from Accra.

The whole atmosphere of our visit had been so different from the slightly stand-off relationship between the team and those people we were associated with Accra, and we experienced a bond with the staff in Kumasi which we had never felt in the capital city. Almost certainly one of the reasons for this was the often repeated complaint that Accra got everything, and Kumasi was left isolated and dragging along on the coat tails of the capital. The obvious pleasure that our visit had given them was a warming experience for the team, and when we were finally ready to depart we all felt quite sorry to be leaving Kumasi, where we had made many friends, and enjoyed the freshness of the weather in this attractive mountainous place.

As we drove towards Accra we agreed that, the next day being Sunday and the admission of the patients for surgery on the Monday having already been taken care of by the staff, we would have a picnic on Labadi Beach, a popular spot on the outskirts of the city, with life guards and adequate rescue apparatus on account of the notorious undertow on the Guinea coast.

After an invigorating, if not entirely enjoyable, swim, with the Atlantic rollers crashing down, and the constant effort to avoid getting swept thirty or forty yards along the beach as each swirling wave passed, we were quite exhausted and lay back on our dry towels – rather foolishly in the centre of the beach, for within minutes we had a succession of vendors trying rather noisily to interest us in a variety of cheap carvings, beads, and yard-lengths of Ghanaian tapestry. Eventually we decided that the middle of the beach was not the wisest place to relax, and gathering our things together, we moved up to the back of the beach.

While we were munching our sandwiches in the shade of one of the string of palm trees fringing the beach, the subject of the lack of trained plastic surgeons in Ghana inevitably came up once again, and someone alluded to the remarks of the Kumasi surgeons regarding the possibility of us coming back some day.

The pros and cons of this were discussed at length, but when I brought up the point about possibly leaving behind more problems than we solved without trained local staff to cope with what were to them unfamiliar problems, the conversation drifted into the possibility of doing something about helping the Ghanaians themselves to become trained to run their own Plastic Surgery Unit in Ghana.

During the next few days the idea of setting up a pioneer Plastic Surgery Unit in the Korle Bu Teaching Hospital, staffed by volunteer surgeons from the UK and Argentina whilst a suitable Ghanaian surgeon was being trained – in English speaking UK because of the language problem – began to take shape. (The term Reconstructive Plastic Surgery came into use when, on a later visit to Ghana, I was speaking at a Rotary Meeting and appealing for funds. At the finish I invited questions, and one individual got up and rather heatedly said he thought it was ridiculous to be asked to donate money for women to have their faces lifted or their breasts made larger or smaller. It immediately dawned on me that the only plastic surgery these people knew about was what they heard about, or saw, on TV or on films – cosmetic plastic surgery. I thanked the questioner, put him in the picture, and as soon as I got back to UK altered our notepaper, at considerable expense, to include the word Reconstructive.)

When we had arrived back in Accra – and the heat – there were messages asking us to check on some of the patients on whom we had operated; but fortunately these were only matters of dressings coming loose, and one patient who had a minor haemorrhage from his head bandage after he had been scuffling with another patient. Things were more orderly this time, and all the patients on whom we were going to operate had been told the day their surgery was booked for, and that they must come in the day before to have a thorough check carried out. This always caused problems explaining why this extra day was necessary, since every day they were in hospital had to be paid for by the patient – no free medicine or medical care being perhaps the most crushing requirement imposed by the IMF.

We were unfortunately losing our team anaesthetist, as, after India, he had only been able to spare two weeks in Ghana, away from his busy practice in Buenos Aires. He was excellent at his job, and although there were other consultant anaesthetists in the Military Hospital, there was no question that, as far as Ghana was concerned, he had been largely responsible for making the surgery flow smoothly during the two weeks he had been with us.

Monday surgery passed off reasonably smoothly once we got used to our new army anaesthetists and the minor difference in their method of working, but we finished rather late on that first day.

On the Tuesday afternoon I was completing my list with a comparatively minor case who, despite our instructions, had only come in that morning, having had some food at breakfast time at 6 a.m. – but who had been starved since then. The patient was a young girl, eight years old, from a very large family, who had had a burn on her right lower eyelid a year ago which had left her with the lid being pulled down a few millimetres, exposing the lower part of her eye. It was a relatively minor procedure to free the shortened lid and fill the raw area so created with a skin graft taken from behind her ear.

I had just started to dissect around the skin graft when she began to cough violently through the anaesthetic tube in her throat, and then, without warning, bought up a cupful of pure pus from her lungs – and began choking. It was patently clear she had a severe pneumonia and her lungs were almost swamped in pus.

The operation was immediately abandoned, and every effort was made to resuscitate the child with oxygen and blind suction. I asked the staff if they had an Intensive Care Unit (as they were called at that time), but apparently they had none. A telephone call to Korle Bu Hospital elicited the fact that their three-bed Intensive Care Unit was not functioning...

One of the army theatre sisters said that she was sure that there was an intensive care bed in the recently-opened Cardio-Thoracic Centre in Korle Bu Hospital – the young, German-trained Head of which I had met during our first week in Accra, and with whom I was most impressed. My urgent call to him had him with us within fifteen minutes. He said he would take the child, along with a nurse and a portable oxygen dispenser, in his car immediately to his Unit, but he was not at all hopeful.

Half an hour later he contacted me to say that the little girl had just died.

It subsequently turned out that she had had a severe cold for some time, which was why they had not come in until that morning, and in some unexplained way her true chest condition was not recognised. When I spoke to her father later he seemed less shocked than I had expected. I put it down to African stoicism; who knows?

As can be imagined, the whole episode cast a deep gloom over the team, but we had to get on with the work on hand during the final three days.

On our last day in the operating theatre, at the end of the week, I was carrying out a repair of a little boy's hand damaged in an accident, and a local TV News crew was filming our team's operating set-up for that night's News. It seemed a God-given opportunity to mention our thoughts regarding the surgical problems in Ghana, and the whole conversation came out on the news a few hours later. By an extraordinary chance the President of Ghana was watching the news that evening, and shortly after it was finished the telephone rang and a lady, whose name I missed, said that the President would like to discuss the matter with the team leader and myself next day. Next day was our last working day, with mountains of people to see and things to do, and I must have inadvertently said something like that because the caller said, rather sharply, `It is the Head of State who wants to see you, Doctor!'

The following evening the whole team, wives included, was driven out to a very attractive mansion at Akuse, on the banks of the Volta river, one of several country residences President Nkruma, the first President after Ghana became independent in 1957, had constructed in various parts of the new Republic.

After the formal introduction to the President (half the members of Parliament appeared to be fellow guests) there was an open-air barbecue, one of my favourite eating experiences, and I piled my plate high with delicious crispy bits of meat, to which I am particularly partial, and sat down at a table to tuck in.

I had barely taken two especially crisp mouthfuls when I was told the President would like Ferriols and me to join him in the Residence. I got up, and without thinking, lifted my plate – which was firmly put down again by the messenger – and along with Ferriols followed him into the Residence and along a corridor to where the President and his small party were seated in armchairs and eating from small side tables. As we came in Rawlings looked up, smiled, and indicated I should sit on the chair next to him. With a nod and a polite smile to the three seated ladies who were also in the room, I sat down. Rawlings smiled at Ferriols and directed to him to sit on a chair beside a very attractive lady, who, I was to find out later, was his wife, the First Lady.

I took a sip of water, as my mouth had become suddenly dry, and waited for Rawlings to open the conversation.

`I heard you saying on the news last night,' he began, `that you and your friends might be able to help us with some of our problem patients, especially the badly burned ones. Tell me about it.'

'We realised, Sir,' I began, `that a team like ourselves, coming here for three weeks and then going off home, can do so little to help your people, and we have a suggestion to make which could provide your people with their own surgeon, or surgeons, who could make a start at dealing with the problem patients you referred to.'

He put his fork down and nodded to me. `Tell me about it, Doctor.'

I then outlined to him the proposal that we would be prepared to train a suitable Ghanaian surgeon in Scotland in the Glasgow Plastic Surgery Unit, and meanwhile we – that is, the Argentine plastic surgeons, and plastic surgeon colleagues in Scotland – could set up a small Plastic Surgery Unit in Korle Bu Teaching Hospital, staffed by a succession of unpaid volunteer plastic surgeons from Argentina and from Scotland, and possibly from other countries. This would mean that when their own man came back at the end of three years training, he would not be faced with what could otherwise be an almost impossible task trying, on his own, to start up a new specialty in a hospital – already in a quandary with surgeons from all other specialties unable to do their job fully because of shortage of beds and theatre space.

He nodded, and looked over at Dr Grant, apparently the lady who had telephoned me, who was his special adviser dealing with all social welfare matters. `He talks about training one of our own surgeons in Scotland,' he said to her. `I thought we had already sent surgeons for this type of training. Where are they?'

`Over the past ten years,' Dr Grant said, hesitatingly, `we have sent three surgeons for training, one to England, but none of them came back.'

Rawlings thumped his fist on the arm of his chair and turned to me. `So what's to stop the surgeon we send to Scotland from staying there and not coming back?' He was obviously not in a mood to hear about the new regulations which reduced the risk of that happening, and equally obviously I had to think up some kind of answer – right now!

`Sir,' I replied, `I would suggest that you choose an experienced surgeon who has made a good position for himself here in Ghana; a married man with a family; and you keep his family here for the three years – we'll send him back on leave from time to time.'

There was a hush over the rest of the room, and he looked steadily at me without a blink. I hadn't the faintest idea what he might be thinking, when suddenly, after what seemed an age but was probably only a minute or less, he started to roar with laughter and grabbed my forearm in his huge hand – I almost yelped with the pain.

`My God, Doctor,' he laughed, `you should be running this country, not me!' And as he laughed again he released his grip. I didn't dare rub the arm, but I moved it out of his immediate reach...

He beckoned Dr Grant over. `This is exactly what I want for Ghana; and I want you to arrange that he is given every assistance to carry it out... And I want to be kept informed what progress is being made!'

When I eventually got back to Scotland I discussed the matter with Martyn Webster, one of my trainees many years back, who thought that what had been decided was an excellent idea, and he volunteered to take charge of the training of the Ghanaian surgeons who we hoped would be coming over.

Three weeks after we had left Ghana I received a fax from Dr Alex Ababio, Deputy Minister of Health, informing me that a suitable surgeon, Dr Fabian Mork – who had actually requested some time before that he might have the opportunity of obtaining some training in Plastic Surgery – would be available to come to Scotland in about five months.

Some time later I learned that, although Dr Ababio had himself made the decision to choose Mork as the prospective trainee, the surgeons at the Military Hospital, strongly supported by the Rotary District Governor, believed that I had made the choice myself – and were furious that I had not chosen one of them.

As a postscript, the reader may be interested to learn that, once we got to know the calibre of the man, we brought Mork's family over to Scotland for a month's holiday – and he did go back to Ghana at the end of his training.

CHAPTER 2

Before the team split up and we went on our separate ways home we had a final discussion about how we would cope with the staffing of the small Unit we were going to establish in Korle Bu Teaching Hospital, which was affiliated with the Medical School in Legone University. Ferriols said he would talk to his peers in Argentina about volunteers coming to help run the Unit in Ghana, hopefully prepared to go out for a month, or even more if it was possible. I promised to do the same in Scotland and England, and wherever there were ex-Canniesburn Plastic Surgery trainees in Europe, and indeed world-wide. This, of course, would require careful co-ordination, and I was sure Martyn would be prepared to handle this.

As far as it would be possible, we would share the fund-raising, although I had an idea that we would probably have to fund most of the costs for the Ghanaian surgeon who was going to be training with us in Canniesburn. For an overseas trainee to be accepted into the regular training programme sponsored by the British Association of Plastic Surgeons, with the status and salary of Registrar, it would involve a lengthy application procedure, and in the present case we needed Dr Mork to finish his training and be back in Ghana to run the Unit as quickly as possible. We had hoped Rotary International would be able to help financially with the volunteers and with Mork, but Ferriols said this would not be possible, and we had discussed the various other options we could take for raising funds.

As far as Scotland was concerned the immediate priority was to establish a Registered Charity, with all the protection and advantages that this would give. With my lawyer, Jim O'Neill, my accountant, John Collins, and Martyn Webster as trustees, the International Reconstructive Plastic Surgery (Ghana) Project was legally registered. And in due course, with talks to Church Groups, Rotary Clubs, and anyone who would listen to The Ghana Story, a start was made to build up the all-important funds.

By an extraordinary coincidence, my membership of the Ayr Rotary Club ceased in mid-January because, being at times involved as a locum for surgical emergencies, my Rotary attendance had fallen below the requisite minimum. Learning about my plan to go out to Ghana just after mid-January, however, Ayr Rotary gave me a letter of introduction to the Accra Rotary, along with a Rotary Friendship Banner.

When Fabian Mork arrived in Glasgow in late August to begin his training, Martyn had already found him accommodation near the

Plastic Surgery Unit in Canniesburn Hospital. He would normally have been accommodated in the staff quarters at Canniesburn – at less cost – but for the first four months there was no spare accommodation available which, apart from the financial side, was a great pity, since he really had no congenial company in his digs and, although the Canniesburn staff did their best to look after him, he was obviously somewhat homesick until he met some Ghanian friends in Glasgow, who ran a Social Club – The Ghana Welfare Association – and invited him to join. Martyn spent considerable time and energy arranging his training, which was not easy as he had no proper job or status, but over the two and a half years he was in Scotland, Martyn went to great lengths to ensure he got a wide training, particularly in the aspects of the work that he would be involved in in Ghana, such as severe burns, which were dealt with in a separate Burns Unit run by the Plastic Surgeons in Glasgow Royal Infirmary.

As the weeks went by I wrote several times to Ferriols. I was first surprised, and then rather worried that I had no word back from him, for there was a lot to arrange, dovetailing volunteers from Argentina with the ones we ourselves were approaching. Then, one never to be forgotten day, a letter arrived, not from Ferriols, but from Ulrich Hinderer, the Secretary of the International Plastic and Reconstructive Surgery (IPRS) Association, to tell me that the Board had been informed that I had been involved professionally in Ghana with Dr Alberto Ferriols, who was not a member of the Argentine Plastic Surgery Society, and had no known training in Plastic Surgery. I was instructed to cease this association immediately or I would be asked to resign from IPRS.

As can be imagined, I was absolutely stunned by this information, but I had been on one of the Committees of the Association for several years when it was first formed, and I immediately telephoned the Secretary, Herr Hinderer, who said the Committee realised I had been conned by Ferriols – he had done this before – and as long as I kept clear of him, there would be no repercussions.

It meant amending all our planning regarding the timetable for those volunteers who had offered to go to Ghana, and looking afresh for new volunteers to fill the places we had left blank on the understanding that the volunteers Ferriols was supposedly gathering would fit into the blanks on the lists I sent him. And it meant that we in Scotland would have to raise every penny we were going to require. The fact that during the time that Mork was training in Glasgow we were able in the end to enlist nineteen volunteer plastic surgeons from seven different countries – many went out more than once to Ghana – is evidence of the prodigious efforts put in to overcome what had at first looked a complete disaster.

When I had more or less regained my sanity, and looked back at the visit of Ferriols' team to Ghana in January, several things began to fall into place. He had never talked about this own training, or indeed about any of his antecedents, and certainly was not acquainted with any of my own South American senior colleagues and friends, or with their particular fields of work. He himself had never operated in Ghana – always giving me the story about being honoured assisting me, particularly with operations I had developed, and I was stupid enough, or perhaps vain enough, to swallow the whole performance without really noticing what was happening. He was a con-man, and a really professional one at that... But the fact of the matter is that if Ferriols had not existed Ghana might still have no Reconstructive Plastic Surgeons.

One of the good things about 1992 was the beginning of my relationship with Eddie Yeboah, Head of Urology and Professor of Surgery in Korle Bu Teaching Hospital. It was a relationship which was to make the setting up of the Plastic Surgery Unit possible, and which I am happy to say continues to this day. I had actually met him two years before at a meeting of the International Plastic Surgery Society in Madrid which he and the then Head of Urology, John Quartey, had attended (despite the fact that neither of them was a member of a National Plastic Surgery Society). Shortly after President Rawlings had commissioned me to set up a Plastic Surgery Unit, Yeboah wrote to me welcoming me and thanking me for what the International Reconstructive Plastic Surgery (Ghana) Project was planning to do for his people. He was very conscious of the gap in the surgical service due to the absence of a Plastic Surgery Unit and had actually tried to set up a unit a year before, in cooperation with Dr Quartey – who had learned to use skin grafts and a few basic skin flaps – but their efforts had not gone far, and, of course, what they had started up had not been intended to deal with the more complex surgical reconstruction problems that called for the ability and experience of a trained plastic surgeon.

One of the matters which Yeboah brought up was the fact that, in Ghana, the Head of any Medical or Surgical Department or Project had the status of Professor, and with the future we were outlining for the Plastic Surgery Project, only a Professor would be accepted as the person in charge.

He wrote asking if I held any Honorary Professorships, and I replied that I held several, mainly in the United States, and suggested he might use the most prestigious one, awarded by New York University – The Kazanjian Professorship – and enclosed copies of the credentials.

These were apparently satisfactory, and thereafter I was addressed in West Africa as Professor, or more usually just `Prof', so everyone was happy and the planning of the Plastic Surgery Unit went ahead, with official recognition.

As the time we were about to start up the Plastic Surgery Unit at the beginning of 1993 drew nearer, John wrote to me saying that he would pass over to me the names of the patients he and Eddie Yeboah had seen, and they would help with starting up the Unit. This gesture, made with the best of intentions, raised a problem which was to recur in the future and lead to some unfortunate situations. When Martyn and I had discussed the formation of a Plastic Surgery Unit in Ghana we agreed that, from the start, it would be run strictly along the lines which would make it acceptable to the IPRS, and to all other official Plastic Surgery bodies. That meant, particularly after the Ferriols incident, that it could only accept properly qualified Plastic Surgeons to run it or to work in it – unless they were trainees – an attitude which Yeboah understood and accepted, but which did not go down at all well with Quartey.

While this correspondence with Yeboah was going on, Martyn had been working on a tentative list of volunteers, and we were concerned that none of the volunteers who had offered to go out in January 1993 to start everything up could go for more than two, possibly three, weeks. Then, out of the blue, by one of the incredible 'coincidences' which marked the whole history of The Ghana Project, the situation was resolved when Chris Bainbridge, one of the Senior Registrars in Canniesburn, who had just completed his training and was about to look for a consultant post, offered to go to Ghana, with his wife and two children, for six months. A coincidence, surely not just by chance, that was to produce a result beyond anything we could have imagined.

We were not to know that Chris and his wife would make, as they did, such a great job of organizing the ward work, the clinics and the operating itself, so that subsequent volunteers were able to slot in, whatever length of time they were going to be there, with a minimum of problems. By the end of Chris's six months, almost all the teething troubles had been resolved, and as well as leaving detailed information regarding running the Unit, he and his wife had actually produced a typed booklet, not only full of sound advice, such as 'Never argue with the Ghanaian staff, they will simply quietly disappear...', but with lists of places to visit, restaurants to go to, and a host of useful information, including a good school for any offspring who might accompany their volunteer parents – as had their two boys.

By the middle of January, when Chris and family were due to arrive, Professor Yeboah had organized for the Plastic Surgery Unit the use of some twenty-five to thirty beds, scattered in ones and twos over several of the surgical wards in Korle Bu Hospital, and had managed to arrange a whole day and a half operating a week in the Children's Theatre block, when most surgeons only had one day a week, and some one day only every two weeks. He had also arranged a hospital villa for them.

Two days after the Bainbridges had arrived and begun getting settled in, I flew out to Ghana, and took a taxi to the Shangri La Hotel, close to the airport and one of the less expensive establishments, where I had booked a room, and was pleasantly surprised to find that the hotel was not the usual featureless square block, but was designed along African lines, with an African village layout. The main part of the hotel, including the check-in and administration offices and the small, almost empty, dining room, was circular in shape, single storeyed – and with the whole of the outside painted white. The central hallway ran right through to a large roofed veranda at the rear of the building where, although I didn't realize it, most people preferred to dine, despite the mosquitoes – which were partly discouraged by a number of large ceiling fans and ultraviolet light insect killers.

The guest accommodation, which was quite separate from the main building, was in the same African style, with round-walled three-bedroomed `huts', with conical roofs, which were dotted in a random fashion about the attractive gardens at the back of the hotel, and all painted white. The concept of it being an African village was certainly achieved, and with African carvings adorning the walls in the main hallway and in the veranda, it made me feel I really was back in Africa. It was certainly one of the most intriguing hotels I have ever come across. There was a large pool, and although I had arrived in the early evening, I put on a pair of swimming trunks and joined a number of other guests cavorting in the coolness of the magnificent swimming pool.

First thing in the morning, I tried telephoning Chris, but the hospital phone system, to put it mildly, was less than satisfactory, and I finally took a taxi across the city to the Korle Bu Hospital, which lay to the west of Accra itself, beyond a rather green-coloured, slow-moving lagoon, where I was able to locate his villa. Chris was not in himself, but his wife told me he was trying to get their luggage released from Customs, as it consisted not only of medical supplies and instruments, but some of their personal baggage with all the children's clothes! To cut a long story short, Chris eventually got in touch with me by phone at the hotel in the late afternoon, almost incoherent with frustration, as he still could not get his baggage released for some unknown reason. I promised to do what I could, though I really hadn't the faintest idea what I could do. When he had finally run out of steam and hung up I told the manageress of the hotel about the problem. To my surprise she said, `I know the very person who can help. At the back of our grounds there is a Polo Club where many ex-pats. from UK go for a drink round about this time. I'll take you down and introduce you to a Scots lady who is one of the personal advisers to the President – she'll know what to do.'

I duly met the lady and explained the problem to her, but before she could reply, a very attractive young lady put a hand on my arm. `I couldn't help overhearing what you were saying: I'll have a word with the President this evening,' she said, `and I'll phone you tomorrow morning. It will be all right, believe me.'

She must have seen the look of astonishment on my face, for she gave me a broad smile and, as she turned back to her companions, one of them, a young man in jodhpurs, pulled me to the side and semi-whispered, `She is a very good friend of the President, so don't worry, everything will definitely be all right: you'll see.'

At eight o'clock next morning I got a telephone call telling me to get some transport from the hospital and, along with Chris, to ask at the Customs Office for the senior officer. We collected a hospital truck and went to the gate of the Customs department where I asked to see the senior officer. When this individual duly arrived he said he had no information about releasing this luggage, and turned to go. I had been told the drill by the young chap at the Polo Club, and I said, in as authoritarian a voice as I could muster, `Get me on the phone to The Castle, please.' (The Castle, originally built several hundred years ago by the Swedes to protect their gold and slave trading endeavours, was today the Headquarters of the President, and the Government Offices, and was the Holy of Holies politically.)

The effect was electrical. The Customs officer straightened up, and stuttering something about a mistake, ushered us with great ceremony to a shed where the luggage was piled on the floor. Our transport was brought through the gates, and several pairs of hands lifted the boxes and suitcases on to it. I was not even asked to sign anything.

Chris very quickly got things started up in the hospital with two surgery registrars allocated to the Unit by Professor Yeboah. And I got on with my job of raising funds.

The strategy I had decided on with regard to this fund-raising, an activity which was totally unknown to me, was to ask the British High Commissioner to introduce me, or give me a letter of introduction, to as many Fellow High Commissioners and Ambassadors as he reckoned might be prepared to help, and then I would ask them to introduce me to business firms, or any other suitable bodies to which I might appeal. When I phoned Mr David Walker, the British High Commissioner, he immediately invited me to come and talk to him as soon as it was convenient – which was as soon as I could get a taxi across to the High Commission! When I was ushered into his office he told me he had learned from the

Dean of the Medical School what the Project was preparing to do for Ghana – and he had been expecting me. On learning I had come by taxi, he phoned the Minister of Health, Commodore Obimpeh, whom he knew well, and the Minister sent a car over to pick me up and bring me across to his office when I had finished talking with the High Commissioner. Obimpeh proved to be a tremendous support for all that I was trying to do, and for the next eight years I always had the use of a Ministry air-conditioned car and driver every time I was in Ghana.

It took me a little while to get my bearings in what was basically for me a totally new country, and not very long after I had arrived back in Ghana Mike Greenstreet, the Deputy British High Commissioner (Mr Walker being temporarily out of the country), invited me to an evening 'drinks and snacks' party being held out of doors in his garden, so that I could meet some of the British community. I had some difficulty locating his house, but when I eventually arrived he was kind enough to break off conversing with a party of Ghanaian diplomats and to take me round and introduce me to one or two of the UK guests, telling them briefly what I was starting up in Ghana. He then got caught up in other matters and I walked round on my own, chatting to one or two people – bringing in wherever the opportunity arose what we were hoping to develop in Ghana.

Eventually a smallish lady came up to me and said she had overheard a little of what I had been saying about setting up something in Ghana, and could I repeat what I had been talking about as she was rather inter-ested. She asked a lot of questions and I was only too pleased to find somebody who was so obviously interested in the Ghana Project. I thought this might be somebody worth cultivating, and I finally said, 'I am sorry; you are who?'

There was a roar from behind my questioner, and Mike Greenstreet, who had at that moment came over to join us, bellowed, 'Good Lord, Jack! this is Lady Chalker!' He turned to her and said, 'I am so sorry, Lady Chalker, I had no idea Jack didn't realize who you were.'

And I really didn't: I had never seen her picture in the papers, and she had none of the airs one generally associates with people of impor-tance – particularly politicians of importance, and she was a Minister of State. She was most gracious about the whole episode, and said she would have a good laugh about it when she returned to London.

Going around with your cap in your outstretched hand asking for donations is no source of joy, and the standard reply I got to my requests for a donation was details of how badly all businesses in Ghana were suffering from the 20 per cent annual inflation rate which was bringing the country to its knees.

One of the few early good results of my begging resulted from my visit to Mr Molenschot, the MD of Shell Oil Company. He listened very patiently while I went through my party piece, and, at the end of it, said, `You are certainly very persuasive, Doctor: if you had been a bit younger I might have offered you a job.' Then he went into the familiar routine about shortage of money. My face must have registered my disappointment, for he quickly went on, `But there is one way we may be able to help you. We have a Guest House for our own staff staying overnight when they come down to Accra on their way to Holland on leave. It is almost never full; and usually it is half empty – and sometimes it is completely empty. I am proposing to give your Project the use of a twin-bedded room, with breakfast, without charge for you and your volunteers when they come out here.'

For a moment I just sat with my mouth open.

`Well?' he asked, `What do you say?'

I pulled myself together. `I say an enormous thank you! Thank you most sincerely! This is the best thing that has happened to us in the whole year. It's wonderful. Thank you.'

`Simply let my secretary have the details of any volunteers proposing to come out,' he went on, `and unless in the unlikely event we were going to be full at that time, the room is yours as long as you need it.'

`Coincidence?' For I nearly didn't go to Shell for help. I had been told by someone that they never gave donations.

Of the diplomatic people I had on my list of individuals to speak to about the Project, one was the Japanese Ambassador, but I had put off seeing him as I had mentally graded the list as `possibles' and `unlikelys', and to be frank, some of the latter I never got round to seeing at all – and the Japanese Ambassador was fairly well down on the `unlikely' list. I had never even seen the Japanese Embassy until one day, looking for the house of a friend to return a book about Ghana which he had kindly lent me, I found myself passing the Japanese Embassy and pulled up at the gate to enquire about my friend's address. The guard at the gate did not know where it was and said he would ask one of the secretaries. He spoke to her on the phone then held it out for me to speak to the girl myself, and as she gave me directions it occurred to me I might ask her about making an appointment to see the Ambassador, so I told her who I was. She spoke to someone else and then asked me if eleven o'clock the following Thursday would be suitable. I said it would be, and thanked her for her help.

It turned out that on the Thursday in question the Ambassador himself was out of the country and his First Secretary received me in his place. One knows, of course, all the clichés about the inscrutable

Japanese, but this official stared fixedly at the wall behind my head and very occasionally said `Ah so' but nothing else, and when I came to take my leave he gave me a very formal bow and handshake, and never looked at me directly in the eyes.

As I walked along the corridor leading from his room, slightly dazed by the experience of talking to a stone wall, a head popped out from a doorway, and a non-Japanese lady asked, in a very welcome Scottish accent, `How did you get on?'

`I really have no idea.' I replied. `I don't even know if he was listening.'

She pulled me into her office and offered me a seat. `Oh yes he was,' she said emphatically. `I am the Ambassador's secretary, and I know the Deputy very well indeed. You wait: although he is not the Ambassador, he is the man who really gets things done. Have a cup of tea. You look as if you could do with one.'

Mrs Evelyn Tay, the lady's name, told me that she came from Edinburgh and that her Ghanaian husband (I subsequently learned he had held an important State position) had died a year ago, which was why she had taken a job as secretary to the Ambassador. She said she, like everyone in Accra, had read in the newspaper about the work we were proposing to carry out for Ghana, and asked me if there was anything she could do to help. I rather stupidly asked if she could type, and she said of course she could, and would be very happy to type anything I needed. She had no idea what a tremendous boon this would be because my writing was so bad that even my secretary at home had difficulty in reading anything I wrote – as I sometimes had difficulty myself. Not only did she type my letters for me, but off her own bat she made enquiries about people I might go to see regarding donations. With her late husband's connections, she seemed to know everybody of importance in Accra, and over the years she became, with Professor Yeboah, officially one of our representatives in Ghana.

Life was beginning to take on a much appreciated upward turn: but there was nevertheless a downside as well...

I was sitting writing in my room one evening when the phone rang and I was told that a Dr Quartey was at the front desk and would like to see me. I told the receptionist to send him along and got my duty-free Macallan single malt whisky (a gift from my son David, who had accompanied me to Amsterdam at the beginning of my journey) out of the cupboard. It had been a pleasant surprise for friends visiting me, and was almost finished.

When he saw the whisky John laughed and said he hadn't tasted a Macallan for years. Gradually the conversation worked round to the subject I had known he had come to discuss – his exclusion from the staff of the Plastic Surgery Unit when, as he said, he had been the one who had really started it. I tried as patiently as I could to explain it was nothing personal, and I even told him about the IPRS letter and Ferriols; but he looked at his almost empty glass, which I hastened to refill with almost the last of the whisky, and went through the whole business again. I tried once more to explain that I was endeavouring to build up something that would be run along internationally approved lines, and be acceptable to the rest of the world. I said that if I accepted him as a part of it, how could I refuse to accept any other surgeon who did a few skin grafts? Finally, the whisky ran out, and I told him I had an early start next day – at which he stood up, a trifle unsteadily as he had had a tendency to gulp my precious Scotch – and without another word he walked out and banged the door shut behind him.

On the second week after I had come out, as already mentioned, I had been invited to talk to the Accra Rotary Club, for which eventuality I had been given a banner by the Ayr Rotary Club to present to whichever Rotary Club I first spoke to in Accra. The chairman, an architect by profession, and a Minister in the Government, on hearing I was very fond of fishing, drove me the following Sunday to a village called Big Ada, situated on the bank of the magnificent three mile wide estuary of the Volta river, to meet a fellow architect, Hein Grüter, from Switzerland, and his wife Ellie, from Holland, who had built a magnificent house right on the shore overlooking one of the most spectacular parts of the estuary, and who was `mad keen on fishing'.

Over the years I went down to the Grüters' house on a Sunday whenever I got the opportunity, and in due course we became firm friends – and caught some fighting barracuda from time to time. I would never have believed that a day would come when our friendship almost foundered as the result of a sequence of happenings over which I had no control, and which almost wrecked the whole future of the Project.

Chris was by now making considerable strides getting a routine started, and increasing numbers were beginning to turn up at his Out-Patient Clinics, some from villages thirty miles from Accra. The progress of the operating sessions, carried out in the more up-to-date operating-theatres of the Children's Block, were a little bit erratic on account of problems regarding a shortage of anaesthetists, but Chris was gradually developing a sufficient amount of stability in his relationships with the Ghanaian medical staff to allow him to get most of the work he wanted to do carried out. One of the disadvantages of the adult operations not being performed in the same building as that in which the patients were housed was the need for them to be transported back semi-conscious from the Children's Block to the main building some distance across a wide roadway: but there was no alternative. The children, however, were housed in a ward in the Children's Block in cots.

As far as my own efforts were concerned, Mrs Tay was proving to be most helpful in introducing me to influential people who had known her late husband well, and gradually, one way or another, contributions – admittedly on a smaller scale than I had hoped for – were beginning to trickle in.

With Chris coping so well I kept out of his way, apart from occasional courtesy calls, and I took the opportunity to go up to Kumasi to discuss with Joe Hiadzi the possibility of the visiting surgeons going up to Kumasi, at least for a weekend, to operate on some of the patients we had had to turn down in 1992 – and perhaps deal with a few new patients. The reaction from the Kumasi staff was very positive, and whilst Bainbridge could not do this because of his family commitments, I assured Hiadzi that we would start the arrangement with the next volunteer.

Around this time a letter was received from a Ghanaian surgeon who, ten years before, had been sent to UK for training in Plastic Surgery, but who for various reasons had stayed on in England at the end of his training. He had heard about the Plastic Surgery Unit now functioning in Korle Bu Hospital, and wrote saying that he would like to return to Ghana and work in the new Unit.

I replied to him saying that I was sure Ghana would welcome him back, but that there were only facilities for one surgeon in the Korle Bu Unit, and I was sure he would be most welcome in Kumasi where he would be able to set up his own Unit. However, he was only interested in working in Accra, where all his numerous relatives lived, and he chose in fact to come back independently to Accra, where the Ministry gave him the post they had originally earmarked for him in Korle Bu Hospital. Some years later, under quite different circumstances, he became one of the staff on the Reconstructive Plastic Surgery and Burns Centre.

A request was also received from another Ghanaian surgeon who had, several years before, gone to Poland to train in plastic surgery. He wrote saying he had heard about the new Plastic Surgery Unit in Accra, and as he was now finished his training in Poland, he would like to come back to Accra and join the staff of the Unit.

He had given me the names of two of his teachers, and I wrote to them, but perhaps the post there was not functioning normally and no replies were received. In any case I had explained the situation to this doctor, Pius Agpenorku, and told him why, as I had done before, it would not be possible for him to be part of the Reconstructive Plastic Surgery Unit in Korle Bu Hospital; and I told him also that I knew he would be made very welcome in the Teaching Hospital in Kumasi. I also said that I would be happy to contact Professor Hiadzi about the possibility of him starting up a Unit there.

Somewhat grudgingly he abandoned the idea of starting up in the busy Metropolis of Accra, and to cut a long story short, he was eventually appointed Consultant Plastic Surgeon in the Komfo Anotye Teaching Hospital in Kumasi in 1994. I asked Fabian Mork to give him sufficient instruments and equipment to enable him to get started, and promised him that any of our people coming out to Accra would visit him for a few days in Kumasi to help with the more difficult cases that he might encounter.

The surgeons in Kumasi were delighted to have their own Plastic Surgery Unit, and when Pius eventually moved up there he was beginning to get quite enthusiastic about starting up this new Unit, and was very pleased that the volunteer surgeons would be giving him a hand with difficult problems.

By the end of February I was due to return to Scotland, and I spent a pleasant last few evenings having dinner with some of the friends I had made. One in particular, Commodore Obimpeh, the Minister of Health, whom I mentioned briefly earlier, had made me most welcome, and the affinity we developed, he having been the Senior Officer in the Ghanaian Navy, and I having been a Medical Officer in the British Army during the war, built up a partly-joking, partly-serious, bond against all the other `civilians' who were perhaps slow in demonstrating the spirit of helping that I was so much in need of with regard to the development of this new specialty in those early days. Without his help matters might have taken a very different course from what eventually became the reality.

One of the most useful things he had done for me was, as I already indicated, the arrangement he had made that I would have the use of a Government air-conditioned car and driver any time I was in Ghana. The drivers varied, depending on who was available, but with only one exception they were good at their job, and they all became friends – so much so that, as the years rolled by, when we pulled up at crossing lights there was seldom a time when a previous driver would not shout over to me, `Welcome, Prof!' from one of the other lines of traffic, despite having a Minister of State sitting behind him.

On my return home to Scotland I found that Martyn had got together a list of prospective volunteers for over a year ahead, so it looked as though we were really on the way with our plans, provided our funds could afford it. Fabian Mork, despite not being the usual type of salaried trainee, was getting a broad surgical exposure, thanks to Martyn, without the tedium of spending half of his time writing up case-notes on patients, as he would have had to do in a regular paid post. Funds were gradually coming in, from UK as well as from Ghana, and without the need to pay for accommodation in Ghana in the future, thanks to Mr Molenschot and Shell, we were fairly sure we could meet the cost of fares and Mork's expenses for the foreseeable future.

Though matters were moving along fairly satisfactorily with the Plastic Surgery Unit in Accra, one constant source of great annoyance, already remarked on, the ever present reminder of the IMF ruling that there would be no free medicine or medical care, made the work of the Clinic doubly difficult – or to be more correct half the time spent examining and talking with patients, or their families, was time wasted since, because of the ruling, it meant that when patients were seen in the Out-Patient Clinic we had to give them an estimate of what their hospital and other costs would be, and effectively this meant that almost half of those who came to the Clinic could not afford the treatment we could offer them, and we never saw them again.

I had by now accepted the fact that I would probably be going out to Ghana every two to three months. And when I next arrived back in Accra at the beginning of April it was a pleasant surprise to find Professor Yeboah and Mrs Tay meeting me at the airport; and even more of a surprise when they steered me into the cool air-conditioning of the VIP lounge, a privilege that was to apply in future to each of us working for the Project, and the various volunteers arrived and left in comfort and in style: a great boon when one thought of the milling crowds filling the main airport and the nearby road space in the tropical heat. Thanks to the generosity to the Ministry of Health, and considerable spade work by Mrs Tay, the privilege exists to this day.

They drove me to the Shell Guest House, to which I had paid a courtesy visit on my previous trip to Ghana, and once there, after a journey which started when I left home at 6 a.m. that morning, I could really relax with my two friends over a drink in the comfort of the almost empty lounge. The Guest House had originally been two back-to-back large private houses, but when Shell purchased the whole building, they knocked down the intervening wall and converted it into one spacious structure which outdid any hotel for sheer comfort. There was a large garden, with guards at the gate, and luxury of luxuries, a swimming pool.

Only once in all the years we were privileged to use it was the Guest House full – for six days – when I went out and 'our' room was not available. The ever-resourceful Mrs Tay had, however, arranged accommodation for me, without charge, for two days each at the three most prestigious hotels in Accra, the Golden Tulip, the Labadi Beach Hotel and the French Novotel, so I had the opportunity of savouring the habitats of the rich and famous – but I was very glad when `our' room in the Shell Guest House became available once more and I could move back. The staff were so friendly and efficient, and it was almost like a home from home, instead of the impersonal experience of staying in a large, bustling hotel full of strangers.

It was certainly interesting to have the opportunity of comparing the three hotels, and good of them to have me as a guest, but knowing no one in a very large hotel is a somewhat difficult position to be in, although it would depend very much on one's own taste. The gardens of the Labadi Beach Hotel opened directly on to the beach via a locked gate with an attendant guard, and mindful of the day I had spent there with the Argentines I asked him to open the gate and took a stroll along the fairly busy beach, remembering the fateful decisions we had made on that day. Sitting down on the sand to watch the bathers, I suddenly found a young Ghanaian girl sitting down beside me.

`Would you like to have a good time, handsome?' she said.

`No thanks,' I replied, getting rapidly to my feet and making a beeline for the hotel gate. `Handsome,' she had called me – she must have been blind, poor soul.

Chris had got things thoroughly organized by this time, and suggested to me that we might consider training a ward nurse and a theatre nurse in Scotland. We discussed the pros and cons of this and I decided the Project should go ahead with his proposition, once I got back home. The outcome of this was that Sister Elizabeth Poku and Sister Susan Banin came to Scotland, to be followed in time by several others. There was a problem, however, for the Glasgow Royal Infirmary staff were not prepared to take anyone from abroad for training unless they went on a fairly long waiting list. Fortunately the Plastic Surgery Unit in Canniesburn Hospital were prepared to take Sister Poku for training, and the Ayr Hospital were prepared to take Sister Banin, so the problem was solved. Later on Arthur Morris organized regular training facilities for several nurses, mostly, it is only fair to say, for the Unit in Kumasi.

As usual I had plenty of visits to make during my stay, for Mrs Tay had been busy making contacts for me to follow up, and at the end of the first week I was relaxing in the Guest House lounge and talking with Shell staff employees who had come down from one of the Shell inland stations on their way home to Holland the following day.

One of the Guest House staff came into the room and said there was a gentleman in the hallway who wanted to see me, so I told her to bring him in. She opened the door wide – and in walked Alberto Ferriols!

As he stood in the doorway smiling round the room, I could hardly breathe, I was so completely stunned. Getting to my feet, I walked over to him. `What the devil are you doing here?' I almost shouted at him, and as he moved towards a chair I put out my hand and steered him back to the door and into a small office along the corridor.

He didn't seem in the least put out, and as I shut the office door he said, perfectly calmly, `I have come to help Bainbridge; and by the way, I am staying at the First Lady's house.'

He smiled at me and sat on the edge of a small table. I was having difficulty speaking at all to the man, and this latter piece of information did nothing to help. Finally I managed to pull myself together enough to practically yell at him, `You can stay where you damn well like, but you are certainly not working here!'

I was getting more in control of myself, and I saw the smile becoming less fixed.

`What about all the funds you were going to raise?' I demanded, `and the volunteers you were going to gather?'

His grin came back. `There were some problems; but I am hoping to get started on it when I go back.'

He shrugged his shoulders and resumed his cocky attitude, and it suddenly dawned on me that he obviously was not aware of the IPRS communication. I told him to wait while I fetched something from my room. He shrugged his shoulders again and I went up to get the copy of the IPRS letter which I had brought with me to show Yeboah and others who had known about the plans made on that Rotary International Visit a year before.

When I handed him the letter he stood up and gradually became paler as the implication of what was said began to sink in.

`What's this all about?' he snorted. `Who the hell are these people? – I've never heard of them...'

`No,' I replied, `that's exactly the problem, for the members of the various Plastic Surgery Associations are all registered with "these people", and as you are apparently not a qualified Plastic Surgeon at all, you are not eligible to be registered.'

By this time I was perfectly cool, and I told him there was no way we could be associated with him, and that I would make it my business to make sure his whole confidence trick was exposed to those who should know more about it. Without replying, he marched out of the door, and I hastened to let him out of the building – but I didn't go back to the lounge. I needed to think how we could counteract any attempt he made to worm his way into playing his con-man tricks on some other gullible individual.

CHAPTER 3

Almost a week had passed since my clash with Ferriols, and having heard no word of him I began to think that he must have been shaken enough to have returned home. I was in for an almighty shock, however, for one of the surgeons from the hospital in Kumasi came down the following weekend on a visit to Accra and by chance we happened to meet on the Monday morning outside the office of the Chief Administrator of Korle Bu Hospital. He told me that Ferriols had arrived in Kumasi – apparently with my approval – the day after I had spoken to him, and he had told Professor Hiadzi that he was going to start up a Plastic Surgery Unit in the Komfo Anoyte Hospital – and gave a talk to the hospital staff on basic Plastic Surgery Principles.

He had formed a Ghanaian Plastic Surgery Association, with himself and Professor Hiadzi as co-founders, and with all the surgical staff in the hospital as members! He had told Hiadzi that he had the personal support of the First Lady, and had made a call to her from Hiadzi's office, with several of the staff present in the room. After four days in Kumasi he went back to Accra en route to Argentina – to raise funds and enlist more supporters, he had said – and had left for Argentina the day before I had received the news of what he had done. I telephoned Professor Hiadzi and told him I was coming up to Kumasi the following day.

On arriving at the Hospital I went straight to Hiadzi's office and gave him the facts. To my surprise he did not react as I had expected he would, and he and his colleagues were not bowled over when I explained the absurdity of the situation; they were obviously delighted at his setting up of a Ghanaian Plastic Surgery Association with themselves as members! Reluctantly I produced the IPRS letter, and showed it to them. At first they were silent with disbelief, but then the discussion – and the shouting – began, and Hiadzi suggested that I should go to a hotel and he would join me later.

When he eventually came to the hotel, he looked very tired indeed, and he flopped down in a chair while I got him a reviving drink. `At first they would not accept that what Ferriols had done was invalid,' he said wearily, but in the end the truth of the situation had begun to filter through, and they finally accepted that they too had been taken in – by a real expert: perhaps also a bit of a psychotic.

I heard later that Ferriols had actually tried his Rotary Plastic Surgery tricks once again, and that this time he had been expelled from Rotary when someone blew the whistle on him – I suspect it might have been the other Argentine surgeon who had been on the original team – and his con trick had collapsed. (The other surgeon on the team in 1992 was in fact a qualified plastic surgeon, but why he had become associated with Ferriols in the first place, I would never know.)

With all the running about the city that I was doing, meeting possible donors, I was gradually becoming familiar with the layout of this fascinating place, and beginning to learn something about its past.

Accra had a history going back several hundred years, to a time when, after the discovery of the Gulf of Guinea by those intrepid sailors, the Portuguese, it was quickly followed by exploratory voyages by ships from other sea-going European countries, and the setting up of trading stations along the extensive coastline of the Gulf.

The discovery that gold and ivory existed plentifully in the lands beyond the coastal fringe led to the setting up of numerous trading stations, largely along the more easterly part of the Gulf Coast, that eventually became known as Nigeria, the Gold Coast, and the Ivory Coast – the latter two as colonies of Britain and France respectively – while the whole Sub-Saharan area, extending right along to the Atlantic Ocean, became known as West Africa.

As the volume of valuable goods in the trading stations increased rapidly there were problems of holding them securely while awaiting shipment back to Europe, and with the deteriorating relationship between the sea-going countries, steps had to be taken to guard them against armed bands of other nationals. The problem became so bad that fortified castles, built usually on rocky prominences, began to appear along the eastern part of the Gulf Coast. With the later advent of the slave trade, originally dealing with tribes of defeated Africans being sold by their African conquerors, and later by Arabs who bought the defeated tribesmen from the conquering ones and then sold them to the Europeans, some of the castles became adapted as prisons to hold the slaves awaiting shipment overseas – mostly to the recently opened up American continents.

Some four hundred years ago a large castle, equipped with cannons to repel attackers from both the sea and the land, was built by the Swedes on a particularly prominent site at a place now known as Accra, but they were eventually overwhelmed by the then rapidly developing British colony, and that area of the Guinea Coast ultimately became known as the Gold Coast.

A small township was developed by the new colonists about a mile westward of The Castle, and was named Jamestown – some of which remains to this day, including the walls of a small fort, and an adjoining prison – while there are still some buildings lining the main street, with verandas on the upper floor which provided shade for the shops below. The whole district is now very run down and poverty stricken, but it seems a pity that no attempt is being made to preserve these historic remains of the birthplace of modern Accra.

In 1957 the Gold Coast became the first colony in the British Empire to achieve independence, under the name of Ghana, with Accra as its capital.

In the Jamestown days extension of the town westward was prevented by a wide lagoon – the Korle Bu Lagoon – which, being over a mile in length, effectively formed the western boundary of the rapidly growing town. Today, bridges have been built across what is now a green, smelly, eyesore, and the land to the west of it has been developed as a mainly African township, with no banking/business sector, but having in its midst the Korle Bu Hospital, the largest in Ghana, much of which was built by the British, with its extensive three mile boundary.

Modern day Accra, if we exclude the Korle Bu District, extends for some six miles eastward of the lagoon, with Kotoka International Airport at its eastern extremity, and is a city of some five million inhabitants, with the downtown business and banking area extending eastwards about a mile from the old Jamestown and encompassing the Parliament House and `Whitehall' State buildings. Whilst some of the banks have four or five floors, there were no skyscrapers to mar the landscape until the end of the twentieth century when a new feature has been the development, eastwards of the banking sector, of a number of fifteen- to twenty-storey business buildings, which look so out of place in a city where hitherto skyscrapers – even moderately high – were totally absent.

Beyond the central business/governmental area lay the sector where all the Ministries were congregated, with their rather drab ochre-coloured four-storey blocks – but beyond that again, the most striking feature of the city is the abundance of trees lining practically every street, and from the air almost obscuring the local buildings entirely, apart from the occasional higher structure, particularly apparent as one moves out eastward into the residential areas.

Many of the trees, such as the very prolific flamboyant trees, carry an orange-red blossom in abundance at certain seasons, and with the absence of spring as we know it in countries with a more temperate climate, one can see orange-coloured blossom, or the less common blue blossom – name unknown to the author – in one or another area during most of the year.

Most of the principal hotels, with the exception of the French-owned Novotel, are situated beyond the business sector with the Labadi Beach

Hotel and sea front right out beyond the city, and bordering on the only safe bathing area within miles, although there is sandy beach along most of the coast – but dangerous because of the strong undertow.

The main residential part of Accra lies on the east of the city, with the Airport Residential District, where the biggest private houses, with extensive walled gardens, are to be found, and here mango and other roadside trees are to be found in abundance, forming such a prominent feature, and giving cooling shade against the furious heat of the equatorial sun.

Apart altogether from the deterioration in the purely aesthetic sense, the beauty of the city is also counterbalanced by the rapidly increasing traffic problem as one approaches, not just the centre of the city, but beginning some quarter of the way in from the outskirts; particularly in the morning, the roads seem to be solidly blocked by traffic. New highways leading direct into the city are being constructed, and have considerably improved the situation in certain areas, but even the new roads seem to be becoming blocked up in the morning rush – using the word rush in its figurative sense...

In calculating a daily programme I tried to carry out my frustrating use of the erratic telephone system during what I considered it to be the worst of the traffic rush hour, but every time I visited Ghana the rush hour seemed to extend further into the morning, which meant any appointments I did succeed in making could in the end be an hour or more out in time. Fortunately Africa is not the UK, and I found that the majority of those I had arranged to see at a specific time, but was an hour or more late (it was almost impossible to contact anyone on a mobile phone during busy times) were most understanding, and it was unusual if I had to plead with a secretary for an alternative appointment. The sight of an exhausted elderly white man more or less crawling up the executive stairs to the Boss's office, appeared to do much to help my Charity pleading – although I may occasionally have exaggerated it a trifle as time went by – but I did carry a spare shirt so as not to look less smart and incompetent as the long day wore on.

At the end of the first week in May, when I was due to go back to Scotland, I went to The Castle to make my customary report to the President on the progress of the work of the Project. When we had finished talking, he walked with me towards the door, and as we reached it he said, `I wish you could do something about the Argentine matter; it's causing problems in my home.' This had caught me by surprise and I didn't know what to say. There was really nothing I could do about `the Argentine matter', for I had only recently learned that at that first meeting Ferriols and I had had with the President, Ferriols had sat talking with the First Lady about cosmetic surgery, and he had apparently invited her to be his guest in Argentina – although not for surgery – an invitation which she had apparently accepted; and after the matter of his duplicity had been exposed he had obviously poisoned her mind as far as I was concerned. In all the years I spent visiting Ghana I only met her personally once – and that was not in Ghana itself, but at a State function in London, where we only shook hands.

Fortunately, I remembered that Rawlings still took pride in holding the rank of Flight Lieutenant in the Ghanaian Air Force, and turning to face him, I said, 'I am a Professional, Sir, as you were, and I cannot continue to associate in the practice of surgery with someone who turns out to be a non-Professional.' All of this sounded a bit lame, but he simply shrugged his shoulders and held out his hand to shake mine. 'Try, anyhow,' he said, 'and safe journey home.'

Before I left for Scotland, I talked to Chris about the possibility of sending the volunteer who would be following him up to Kumasi for a long weekend to see a few patients and carry out some surgery. Chris's children went to school in Accra, and as I mentioned earlier, he was not in a position to take on Kumasi visits himself, but he thought it was a good idea. I telephoned Professor Hiadzi and told him what we were planning to do, and that I would start the ball rolling with a visit there on the next occasion I was in Ghana. He discussed the idea with considerable enthusiasm, and I was greatly relieved that, since there had been rumblings that we had conveniently forgotten our promises to include Kumasi in our plans, what might have led to a stand-off, unhelpful to everybody, had been averted.

On my return home, I found amongst the large pile of letters to be answered one from a Mr Rex Cook, a Past President of the Rotary Club in Helensburgh, some twenty miles downriver from Glasgow. He had been a guest at the Ayr Rotary Club when I had spoken there some weeks before, and he asked me if I would be prepared to speak to the Helensburgh Club, who met at a hotel some three miles beyond Helensburgh. It would have meant a round trip of roughly a hundred and fifteen miles: but in the end, against my better judgement when I thought about it, I said I would be 'delighted'; a decision that was to have a profound effect on our Project over the next six years.

Rex Cook turned out to be a hyperactive, restless character, who, since selling off his not-inconsiderable paint business, was looking around for something to occupy himself with. He had not only been President of his Rotary Club, but at one stage he had been District Governor of Rotary for the West of Scotland, so he was finding his present status gave him little opportunity to exercise his considerable organising skills. He asked me if I could let him have copies of some of the coloured slides I had shown at the Rotary meeting in Ayr (with examples of patients who had been operated on in the Reconstructive Plastic Surgery Unit in Accra) as, provided I had no objection, he would like to make the work of the team known to other Rotary Clubs, and would ask them to contribute to our Charity Funds.

This was something I had never contemplated, and I was a little hesitant about giving him a set of slides, but by a curious coincidence, I happened next morning to bump into one of the Ayr Rotarians who had been at school with me, and we started chatting over a cup of coffee. Eventually we got round to Cook's proposition, and seeing my hesitation about it, my friend told me Rex was a real live wire, and if he said he was going to get funds for us he would definitely do it.

Rex got his slides, and over the next six years, until his untimely death in the Centenary year, he went out to Ghana several times with me and was a major source of funding, thanks to West of Scotland Rotary's generosity – and to Rex's invincible way of handling people. I am happy to think that Rex considered himself `one of us,' even though his name did not appear on the notepaper.

On one of the occasions on which I took him with me to Ghana we went up to Kumasi, and Hiadzi managed to arrange an audience with the Asantahene, who talked for quite a time with Rex about his Rotary work in Scotland, and the help it was giving to the Project. Generally the Queen would have been sitting by the side of her husband, but on this occasion she was not present, and after I had introduced Rex, I was shaking the King's hand when, to my surprise, he didn't release his grasp but sat down on his throne, still holding my hand. I didn't know quite what to do, but his grip never relaxed and I felt that all I could do was to leave my hand in his until he let it go. I was somewhat embarrassed, standing up beside the seated King, but none of the courtiers and others present seemed to even notice the unusual situation.

Only when, twenty minutes later, his official interpreter (who actually had had nothing to interpret as the King spoke perfect English – he had been to University in England in his younger days) announced that the audition was now ended, the king briefly laid his other hand on top of our closed hands, and then let my hand go.

When the Chamberlain had led us out into the main corridor, he was obviously disturbed in some way, and once we were out of earshot of the Royal Audience Room, he turned to me and, almost in a hushed voice, said, `I have never seen him hold someone's hand for the whole audience – but, of course, the Queen's throne is usually occupied.' He shook his head and looked at the others gathered nearby – `But a white man!' he exclaimed, and turning to me, almost accusingly, said, `It is the greatest honour he could pay you! I know he values the work you and your colleagues are doing to help his people – but a white man! I never heard of this happening in all the years he has been Asantahene – not even when the Prince of Wales was here.' (There was a photograph of the Prince of Wales shaking hands with the Asantahene during a State visit to Ghana, which I had noticed on the wall behind the throne, and when an opportunity had arisen later on I mentioned the photograph to the Prince. He said he remembered that visit to meet the Asantahene very well, and asked me to convey his kindest regards to him – which I duly did.)

Rex had been intrigued with the whole episode, and told half of the population in Accra about it when we got back – which did not go down very well in every quarter, since most of the coastal population were from the Ewe Tribe (pronounced Evy), formerly enemies of the war-like mountain-country Ashanti.

Martyn had by now drawn up a list of firm commitments from prospective volunteers for two years ahead, including some of the consultants from Canniesburn Plastic Surgery Unit, some from England, and quite a number of young men from other countries who had worked at some stage in their training in Canniesburn PSU.

The first volunteer, as it turned out, was a plastic surgeon from Bilbao in Northern Spain, Dr Antonio Barrio, who Martyn and I had come to know very well at the Annual Plastic Surgery Conference, held every year in Vitoria in Northern Spain. (To be perfectly frank, apart from the privilege of `imparting knowledge', one of the chief attractions of this annual meeting was the obligatory two-day visit we made at the end of the Conference, as guests of Dr Antonio Ortega, one of the chief organizers, to a fishing village on the northern coast of Spain where, practically speaking, for almost forty-eight hours we feasted on lobsters, crabs, shellfish of every description, and other oceanic tidbits – washed down with a plentiful supply of excellent Spanish wine...)

When Dr Barrio, and his wife Margaret, eventually went out to relieve the Bainbridges in mid-June, they were delighted with the Shell Guest House, and found a well-ordered Reconstructive Plastic Surgery Unit, with sufficient instructions regarding running it to make it a straight-forward matter. So they had plenty of occasion to bless Bainbridge and his wife who had written up everything that their successors were likely to need to know, including places to visit, in their booklet. Mrs Barrio was English, and had been a nurse, so she gave a number of informative talks to the nurses working in the Unit about the special problems that the nursing of the patients in a Plastic Surgery ward might involve.

Although Chris had hired a small car for himself and his family, it was obvious that the Project would need to purchase a vehicle for the stream of volunteer surgeons who would be coming out. A Nissan pick-up seemed the most useful vehicle and was duly purchased. I discussed the situation with the Minister of Health, and he allocated a driver who would go on the staff of the Unit – although continuing to be paid by the Ministry – starting at 8 a.m. and. finishing at 5.30 p.m. every evening. Fuel and maintenance were also paid for by the Ministry.

The car was for the exclusive use of the current volunteer, and if he wished to use it in the evening or at weekends it was up to him to reimburse the driver. Stories that the car was occasionally seen in town in the evenings with someone other than the surgeon on board were discounted as mere fabrications – or something like that...

Before Dr Barrio arrived I had been in touch with Professor Hiadzi in Kumasi to arrange again for a number of the patients who had been seen by the team in January 1992, but on whom we had not been able to operate, to be brought back for reassessment (as he had already done when I had gone to Kumasi myself) and to add any new problem cases they had encountered, now that we were going to have a regular operating session when the volunteer surgeons visited Kumasi, starting with Dr Barrio.

This arrangement was welcomed by him and the volunteers who followed him, as it meant a break in the routine, and an opportunity to visit a place as interesting historically, as well as geographically, as Kumasi; and the nucleus of a loosely classified Reconstructive Plastic Surgery Unit was gradually built up there over the course of time.

Martyn himself was not able to go on to Ghana until the following year, but the other of my erstwhile Canniesburn trainees, Arthur Morris, who was now Chief of the Plastic Surgery Unit in Ninewells Hospital, Dundee, went out later in 1993, and on a regular basis after that. A Rotarian himself, during the working visit he made to Kumasi with his wife Vicki – herself a trained theatre sister – he spoke to the local Rotary Club, as I had done on that first visit to Ghana in 1992.

Arthur's Kumasi visits, which he began to make every time he went out to Ghana, were eventually to lead to developments we could not have envisaged in those early days, and a synopsis of what he set up, after the Project committee – of which he had become a member – authorized him to do so, with the help of the Ghanaian plastic surgeon who eventually joined the staff in Kumasi, follows later.

With a succession of extremely capable volunteers ensuring the continuous presence of a visiting surgeon, I decided to cut down on my own visits to Ghana, unless to deal with something that required my presence, particularly if the Ministry was involved, to around two weeks every three months: spending more time writing to possible donors in the UK, telling them what the Project was all about, and asking for donations. Admittedly not as effective as speaking to people face to face, but it was surprising how much interest it did evoke – and it was a lot less taxing to carry out. And to be frank, although she never complained, three weeks on her own every three months was a bit unfair on my wife. (When I finally retired, she reckoned I had spent two years of our married life in Ghana.)

One of the pleasanter duties I had been involved in in 1993 was to accept, on behalf of the Project, the valuable gift of a $45,000 operating microscope from the Japanese Ambassador, whose deputy had seemed so uncooperative, on behalf of the people of Japan – a great boon in modern reconstructive plastic surgery, and an almost essential piece of equipment in today's advanced micro-vascular techniques of tissue transplantation.

And thereby hangs a tale...

Apart from the operating microscope, the Japanese had made one or two other donations of equipment to the Project, but when a new Ambassador was appointed in the summer of 1994, Mrs Tay sent me a fax saying that she had made an appointment for me to meet him on my forthcoming visit, `as he is very different from the last one.' When I did eventually meet him, he looked to me exactly like the last one, if a little stouter, and when I got the same stone-wall reception, I felt I was wasting my time. I was trying to think of a way to end the unsatisfactory interview, when the Ambassador suddenly said, `You Scottish man? I know Scottish song – the Bonnie Banks of Lock Lomon.' And he gave me a broad, un-Japanese smile!

To say I was astonished at the way the interview was going would be a gross understatement, but I rallied sufficiently to say, `I know a Japanese song myself...'

`A Japanese song?' he queried, and this time it was his turn to be astonished.

`Which song you know?'

So I began to sing a song a little Japanese boy I had known at school had taught me – 'Ya marano naa Kano...' and to my complete surprise the Ambassador joined in – to the obvious disbelief in what he was hearing, of his First Secretary, who had probably never seen his boss smiling, far less heard him sing – and with a foreigner to boot! As one might imagine, this led to a very amicable situation, with Japanese tea being brought in with due ceremony, a situation which, in the course of time, was to play a signal part in helping us achieve objectives we had not even contemplated at that stage. (This was the second time singing my Japanese song had produced unexpected benefits. In 1968, the year when the big Tet Offensive took place in Vietnam, I had been invited by an American surgical colleague to help in the setting up by the Americans of a Children's Plastic Surgery and Burns Hospital in an empty tenement building in Saigon, with the ground floor being the working part of the set up, whilst the floors above were turned into the wards, and the very top flat housed the staff sleeping quarters. While I was there, I met a Japanese neurosurgery team at a Vietnamese party where the custom was that everyone had to do a `turn'. When I sang the song, the Japanese surgeons joined in, amidst lots of laughter, and subsequently gave me a helping hand with a number of head injury cases.)

As the months extended into a year, and then another year, the efforts of the unbroken succession of enthusiastic and hard-working volunteer surgeons, sometimes under very difficult conditions, began to produce a Unit which was recognised – and valued – by the surgical fraternity in Korle Bu Hospital, and also in the Medical School in Legone University; and behind this visible development lay the continuing efforts of Professor Yeboah and Mrs Tay, now joined by Mr Alex Kujiku, a quantity surveyor, and previous Rotary President. I had met him at a communal friend's house, and he had shown a great interest in what we were doing. In course of time he became not only a very good friend, but more importantly, an official Project helper, in which capacity he proved invaluable. Working behind the scenes most of the time, he was able to overcome many of the problems that had to be addressed.

Over the years Alex and I became close friends, and often at weekends he would take me in his car to visit places of interest, and occasionally to take part in local events which I would never have been able to do on my own. On one occasion he took me to a funeral service being held in a church some twenty miles from Accra. The person who had died was a well-known Ghanaian doctor, who had been a great philanthropist (there were posters with his picture, announcing his death, all over Accra) and at the well-attended outdoor service held in a large area in front of the church where his embalmed body lay, there were eight local Chieftains, with their retinue of attendants, each carrying his staff of office topped with the particular gold decoration denoting his function. The gowns and head-dress worn by the various chiefs and their attendants were highly decorative, and the large number of them gathered together like this created a striking spectacle.

When the oration bad been given in the local dialect and the minister had withdrawn into the Church, the mourners began to troop up to the entrance to the church, headed by the senior chieftain and his attendants and followed by the other chieftains in what was obviously a strict order of seniority. When the last of the chieftains had disappeared into the building with their retinues, after a due pause, the rest of the mourners walked up the steps and into the comparative darkness of the church. The slow movement through the church and up past the open coffin, with the upper part of the embalmed doctor discreetly displayed, wearing a dinner jacket and bow tie, is something I will never forget, and I felt privileged to be a part of it – the only white person there as far as I could see.

A new problem was beginning to arise concerning the running of the Unit which we never foresaw, for with the gradual increase in patients, both old and new, coming to the weekly clinic, the numbers were becoming almost more than could be coped with in a half day session once a week – which was without question as much as the overworked Hospital was able to allocate to the Reconstructive Plastic Surgery Unit. Ironically, the IMF restrictions mentioned earlier regarding there being no free medicine or medical care, meant that about half of the patients seen in the Clinic did not turn up for surgery – and so did not appear later at the Clinic for follow-up, which at least helped to keep the numbers down: but for the wrong reason. We were later to realize that, unless for some unusual circumstance, patients who had been operated on did not come back for follow up because of what it would cost them. Irritating as this was, it was even more disrupting to have patients not turn up for their surgery, with an unfilled blank left on the operating list.

This problem was brought home to me for the first time by a partic-ular incident involving a baby with a severe cleft lip and palate which were interfering with its feeding, and who was brought to the clinic by the distressed parents.

We had arranged for the child to be operated on a week after we saw it, but when the time came the mother and baby did not turn up. There was nothing we could do about it, for patients living in country districts, like this family did, often had no verifiable address, but about three months later I was having a look at the patients in the wards when the nurse who was showing me round said of one of the patients who had had surgery to an injury involving his right leg, `This is the father of the little girl with the cleft lip and palate who you were saying had never turned up for surgery. I remember him because I was on clinic duty that day.'

I asked the man why he had not brought his little girl back for surgery, and he said, `I have two cows, whose milk is about all we have got to feed our four children, and the amount which the hospital told me her operation would cost would have meant me selling one of the cows to pay for it – and I could not do that just to pay for one child's operation, though I may now have to do it to pay for my own treatment here.'

We were all taken aback at the realization of just what the IMF regulation actually meant in people's lives, and in discussion with Martyn Webster it was agreed that the Project would, in this particular instance, pay for the child to have its cleft lip and palate repaired – only paupers could be treated free.

In due course I related the facts of the little girl's case to President Rawlings, who was so moved by the situation the poorer people in his country were placed in by the rulings of the IMF that in due course he was to bring this up publicly in a manner that brought the Project directly into the whole problem.

One other acute problem, which affected all the hospital surgeons, was the shortage of anaesthetists and whilst Professor Yeboah had, against much resistance, arranged that we should have the use of some twenty-five to thirty beds, and a day and a half in the operating theatre, this was a constant problem over which he had no control, and some of the volunteer surgeons brought their own volunteer anaesthetist with them.

Shortly before Mr Mork was due to return in early 1995 to take up his post as Surgeon-in-Charge of the Unit (he had meantime qualified as a Fellow of the Royal College of Surgeons of Edinburgh, which in the British convention entitled him to drop the ordinary prefix Doctor and to be known as Mr Mork), I was making one of my tri-monthly visits, and the wife of the volunteer surgeon in post phoned me about six o'clock one morning to say that I would have to cancel the operation list for that day, as her husband had been up all night with severe diarrhoea, and could not possibly operate. With the problems we had had to get an anaesthetist for the day's surgery, I told her we could not cancel the list but not to worry – I would do the operating myself. Accordingly, two years since I had last held a scalpel in my hand, I got my sleeves rolled up (figuratively speaking) and tackled what turned out mostly to be taking skin grafts from one part of the patient to put onto a raw surface on another part, and I managed to get through the whole lot; but the list took much longer than it should have done in ordinary circumstances!

Later that afternoon, I had an update meeting with President Rawlings and, as I walked rather wearily into his office, he greeted me with, `You are looking tired, Doctor,' as we shook hands.

`I am tired, Sir,' I replied. `With all our patients scattered in ones and twos spread over the six surgical wards; the lifts not working and no air-conditioning, (open windows being the British builders' legacy) I am tired.'

He got up from his seat and came over to a chair near where I was sitting. `But this is ridiculous,' he exclaimed, almost angrily – as if it was my fault, `You should have your own building, with your own wards, your own theatres and your own clinics: everything in one building!'

`That would certainly be ideal, Sir,' I replied. `But who is going to build it?'

He pointed his finger at me, almost touching my chest. `You!...' he exclaimed, and I was so flabbergasted I couldn't think of a reply. `My Government will help,' he went on, `and I am sure you will find businessmen and Embassies who will help. Tell them it's my idea!'

Once I had got over the initial state of surprise and shock I had felt as I tottered down the stairs to my car, I began to look at the problem of how to go about this matter, on which the President was obviously serious.

I had discussions with Yeboah, and then with Alex Kujiku, who initially had an architect friend draw up sketch plans for a twenty-four bed Unit which could be constructed in a space between two of the Korle Bu blocks of wards; only to be told this could not be permitted since there were pipes running under the site – though this did not stop someone else putting up a building there the following year! I also discussed the matter with various others, and it was the consensus that, with our own operating theatres, we could handle twice the number of beds we were using at present, and fifty-eight beds with two operating theatres would be the figure to aim at. Finally I went to see my architect fishing friend, Hein Grüter, to ask for his advice.

`Firstly,' he said, `we need to know how many beds you think you are going to need, and how many operating theatres you would require. Once you decide on these points I'll draw up a rough plan for you.' Unlike myself, he took the whole thing in a very matter-of-fact manner; but he didn't have to worry about getting it paid for...

Professor Yeboah, however, brought up a problem: `There will be a great deal of jealousy among the other surgeons; and if it was possible to help them cope with their own surgical problems, for instance the chronic leg ulcers they have so much trouble with, it would go a long way to keep everyone happy – or happier.'

I thought about this, and asked him how many beds that would mean.

`Six male and six female beds, which the other surgeons would look after, would probably solve the problem,' he replied.

`That would be seventy beds!' I exclaimed in alarm. `How on earth could we raise enough money for a building that size?'

No one had an answer to that question and we sat glumly thinking about the problem.

`What about the old Chest Diseases building?' someone queried, `It's got at least that number of beds, and has been standing empty for goodness knows how long.'

I discussed all this with Hein, and a few days later he showed me a tentative plan he had drawn up, using all the available space, for a sixty-bed unit, with two operating theatres. The suggestion that we might renovate and perhaps make some modified alterations to the old Chest Diseases wards, appealed to him, and he asked me to let him know if we could get permission to use the building. When I spoke to the Minister of Health about renovating the old building, he told me that in fact this very point had been raised in Committee and was about to be agreed on as our Reconstructive Plastic Surgery and Burns' Unit.

Hein was given an old plan of the building which one of the hospital engineers had dug up from somewhere, and he duly drew new plans showing some of the walls being knocked down to make bigger wards. He finished up with a seventy-two bed unit, to include three beds for prospective private patients – but without operating theatres, as the Government surveyors considered large sterilisers would not be suitable in the old building, which meant we would have to ferry the patients to and fro between the Unit and one of the general surgery operating theatres.

I explained to the Ministry that it would be quite impracticable, and even dangerous, for patients recovering from an operation to be moved about in this manner, possibly before they had fully recovered from the effect of the anaesthetic. After prolonged discussion – and argument – I was informed that permission for a separate new building would be granted, with the Government contributing towards the cost, but it being my responsibility to raise the balance!

Hein very patiently drew a third set of plans, and produced drawings of a magnificent building, with sloping tiled roofs, and broadly speaking in the general configuration of a Capital H, with an administrative block bridging horizontally across the foot, and totally different from the usual concept of a flat-roofed rectangular block, identical with all the other rectangular blocks that make up conventional old-fashioned hospital buildings. It would include, apart from the double operating theatre suite and recovery ward, the twelve beds for the leg ulcer patients that the general surgeons would be looking after, plus three beds for private paying patients, and I informed the Minister that we were now ready to get started on the Reconstructive Plastic Surgery and Burns Centre – for Professor Yeboah and I fully intended that it would become a Centre of Excellence in due course.

A few days later the Deputy Minister of Health, Dr Adibo, asked me to call at his office. Once I was seated he opened a file lying in front of him and handed me a sheet of paper with three names on it. 'These are the names of three firms of architects from which you can choose – the first one is reckoned to be very good.' Hein Grüter's firm was not on the list, and I snapped over at the Deputy Minister, `I already have an architect, and he has produced all the plans and working drawings needed to construct a building as soon as the Ministry allocates the site.'

`I am sorry,' broke in Adibo sharply, `but we don't work that way: you have to choose one of these three. After all, the Government is paying for it, so it makes the regulations.'

By now I was getting really angry, and if he hadn't been on the other side of the desk I might have shaken the little man. `I'll take this up with the Minister!' I spluttered, `This is ridiculous...'

`The instructions are from the Minister,' he said calmly. `and that was the instruction he was given. He is in his office right now if you want to go and talk to him.' I was so angry I decided it might be better not to see the Minister, at least not at that moment, in case I lost my temper again – which would have been a fatal error, leaving any future discussions jeopardised.

What on earth was I to say to Grüter? And in any case, how was I to know the best firm to pick? After giving it some thought I considered that the best thing would be to get the Grüter part over as quickly as possible; for all I knew he might take the matter to Court. With justification!

Crossing the room in his block of studio offices, Hein put out his hand to shake mine. `So how are things going?' he asked cheerily.

I could have sunk through the floor `Hein,' I said huskily, `There's been a dreadful mix up...' And I began to tell him what had happened.

He was understandably livid. `I thought you had clearance from The Castle,' he stormed. `Why don't you go and see your friend Rawlings?' He sat down in a chair and stared at the ceiling. `I just can't believe it!' he kept on repeating.

I had no idea of what to say, and after he had finally stopped saying anything I thought it best to make a final apology and then leave.

It was six months or more before he contacted me, and to my surprise and intense relief, he rang me one day and asked me if I'd like to come fishing that weekend at Big Ada. `I caught two barracuda last weekend,' he said. `They are all over the place!' The relief was enormous, for we had been really good friends, and I later learned that his wife Ellie had talked him gradually into accepting that it was not my fault, and there was nothing else I could have done.

In the meantime I had to get on with the business of deciding which of the three architects to choose. When I had realised there was nothing I could do about employing Grüter, I told the Minister that I would only continue with the matter provided I could use Grüter's design, whoever got the contract. And I have to admit, to my surprise this was eventually agreed.

Curiously enough, I was getting suggestions from various people in the Ministry and elsewhere that I should choose a particular firm (I later learned that the head of the firm held an important position in the local branch of the ruling Political Party), but he seemed a reasonable enough person when I went to see him at his office; and anyhow, I realised that there was nothing I could do about it, even if he had been a thoroughly unpleasant, ugly individual.

His own senior architect was not at all keen on using Grüter's plans, and altered the ground floor quite drastically. Fortunately, this was his undoing. He was obviously totally inexperienced in designing a hospital, and he had followed Grüter's plans after a fashion, but the unsterile rest rooms and the sterile theatre block communicated directly, while at the far end of each of the two operating theatres there was an exit door opening onto the unsterile corridor – so that patients could be quickly removed!

But the *pièce de résistance* was the inclusion of a mortuary, opening halfway along the main administrative corridor!

It was clear to everyone that he hadn't the slightest knowledge of hospital lay-out with regard to sterility and non-sterility. But the inclusion of a mortuary within the building, particularly such a small building, was the main damning factor – no one would have gone within fifty yards of it, nor, in reconstructive plastic surgery, was there a significant mortality rate; but even so, hospital mortuaries are discreetly situated well out of sight of the main building wherever possible.

So Grüter's plans were accepted, somewhat unwillingly in some quarters, but with no more argument, and he was credited publicly with the design of what was to become the Reconstructive Plastic Surgery and Burns Centre, which would be admired by everyone who saw it. The incident of the altered design, however, was only a foretaste of the problems that eventually lay ahead.

By this time I was thoroughly exhausted, and I decided to spend the last two days of my stay up in Kumasi, away from the whole frustrating business.

From my earlier brief visits I had learned that there was much of interest to see in this attractive hill city, and after checking in at the main hotel, I paid a visit to the historic Fort, built in the late nineteenth century by the British. In 1900 the then British Ambassador, involved in a serious dispute with the then King of the Ashanti People, had marched from Accra up to the Royal Palace in Kumasi and forcibly removed the Ceremonial Gold-covered Royal Stool on which the Monarch sat at the head of a circle of his vassal Chiefs, each sitting on his own much less ornate stool, in Council.

This incredibly stupid thing to do, bringing shame on the King, led to an ugly situation developing, from which the Ambassador escaped by the skin of his teeth into the security of the Fort. A messenger managed to slip out of the Fort at the last moment with orders from the Ambassador to the British Commander in Accra to march as quickly as possible to rescue him and those who had managed to reach the safety of the Fort.

This the army eventually did, but it led to the Third Ashanti War, in which, as already related, the Ashanti were again defeated. It was fascinating to walk round the wooden battlements, with the original field guns still in place at each protruding angle of the battlements, and when I went into a large hall, which had been turned into a museum, I was astonished to come across a copy of the *Glasgow Herald* dated 20 February 1901, with the story of the Ashanti defeat – some fifteen years before I was born.

The city itself was most attractive, with hundreds of jacaranda trees covered in red blossom, which, as one approached the centre, gave way to the usual congested urban sprawl, the main feature of which, in Kumasi, is the bustling chaos of what is reckoned to be the biggest open market in Africa.

Standing on the pavement of a small rise in the main road coming into the city, I was able to look down on the seemingly endless rows of booths and open-air stalls, which stretched into the distance until one could hardly see the furthest part of the market. To walk in its crowded lanes, as I eventually did, with the noise and the bustle, and the cries of vendors ringing in one's ears, was quite a unique experience, even if ultimately it was a relief to escape from it. Every possible market item one could possibly think of, from pots and pans to skilfully fashioned African carvings in a variety of hardwoods, of people in natural as well as in abstract forms. There was a variety of carvings of animals, particularly elephants, which came in all sizes from one inch high (smaller even than the ones we had seen in Adda) to really gigantic monsters that would have taken a crane to lift – or about ten men – and it was difficult to resist buying something, but I already had a houseful of Ghanaian carvings and other mementos of the years I had been going back and forth to Ghana, and I had been given a strict injunction that no more Ghanaian mementos were welcome.

Further along there were ceramic pots of every shape and colour, along with ivory carvings, silver figures, and time expired weapons of every kind, from native assegais and clubs to rusty old army rifles, just as in the market in Accra, and of course, most colourful of all, a whole streetful it seemed of the varieties of the beautiful Kente cloth. It was just a repeat of the market in Accra, on a much bigger scale. And yet there was still a fascination just walking along, looking and listening – and smelling – something that only Africa can provide.

In the afternoon I visited the National Park, which is virtually an open-air museum, with displays, under shelters, of Royal costumes for both men and women, from the past century and a half, and something I found most intriguing of all, an open-air smelting workshop where, using the Lost Wax technique, bronze figures of historic Africans or purely imaginary subjects are made, first of all being carved in wax, then coated with a two inch layer of plaster of Paris, with small holes to prevent air entrapment, and leaving a funnel-shaped aperture at the top into which molten bronze is poured, burning out the wax. Once the plaster has cooled significantly, it is carefully broken up and removed, leaving an exact copy of the wax original. The technique is known the world over, and is thousands of years old, but this was the first time I had actually seen it carried out.

The following morning, on the advice of the manager of the hotel at which I had been staying, on the way back to Accra, instead of leaving the city by the usual route, we took a different road which ran through the heart of several mountains south-east of Kumasi, and after driving about fifteen miles through the most beautiful rugged scenery, we suddenly came through a small gorge and found ourselves looking down into an enormous, more or less circular, amphitheatre, surrounded on all sides by mountains, and about four miles across. As we moved forward to begin our zig-zag descent into it, we could see a large lake, itself some three miles wide, glistening down at the bottom of what we now realized had been, millions of years ago, the crater of a gigantic volcano which our hotel manager had told us about – but had omitted to tell us its size.

As we neared the water of the lake, the sparse mountain vegetation began to change into a thick carpeting of flowers that spread all round this hidden lake, the water of which was as clear as glass, and with hardly a breath of wind to ruffle its surface. As far as I could tell, there was no one else there, and the quietness and stillness gave the place a feeling of awe one might experience in a mighty cathedral. I sat for almost an hour drinking in the quietness and the peace – letting the worries awaiting me in Accra melt away as if somehow they had all been solved.

The lake, I learned later, was called Bosumiwi, but I never found out if that had a special interpretation behind it. I felt sure it must.

One encouraging matter was the progress that Fabian Mork was making in dealing with the ever-increasing number of patients he had to operate on; and he welcomed the volunteer surgeons' visits for around a week every three months to assist with complicated cases.

CHAPTER 4

On my previous visit to Ghana in the latter part of 1995, which ended up so chaotically over the construction of the new Centre, I seemed to have been seeing a different side to Ghanaians, or at least to some Ghanaians, than I had hitherto been used to. I suppose the people with whom I clashed over the matter of who made the decisions regarding the building of the now Reconstructive Plastic Surgery and Burns Centre were only doing their job, but their manner, and the handling of the situation, was certainly off-putting.

That experience aside, I had always found the ordinary people of Ghana to be amongst the friendliest it has been my good fortune to meet. It was not just a question of their attitude that I found intriguing, but I found even their dress, at least that of the women, was so much brighter than the drab apparel of most of the women in so many African countries I had had the opportunity to visit.

It was fascinating to see the women in their many-coloured blouses, with their billowing sleeves and matching turbans, and although these were far from looking like work-a-day garments, they seemed to be worn everywhere, at least in the cities.

The extremely practical way the mothers amongst them carried their babies strapped face forward to their backs in a huge shawl, with two little bare feet sticking out in front on either side, was something I had never seen before, but it was an extremely practical way to carry your baby and leave your hands free to be busily involved washing clothes, or weaving the lengths of Kente cloth so eagerly sought after by tourists – and the Ghanaians themselves, for every situation where a strong, decorative fabric was needed.

The men, even though relative strangers, would say 'God bless you,' or some such friendly words when leaving you if you had been speaking to them; and they would invariably shake your hand on leaving you with a curious sideways sliding away of the hand which I mistakenly thought to begin with was some kind of Masonic gesture. Once I realised it was simply the Ghanian manner of parting, and had finally, after much rehearsing, mastered it, the person whose hand I was shaking would laugh and say, 'You are now a real Ghanaian!'

But it was the children who gave one an insight into the Ghanaian temperament. We came in contact with them of course in the hospital wards as patients, in the rather unnatural circumstances, but the normal behaviour of children could scarcely be judged from that. Kids in the city were active and bright, and almost always were trying to sell you something, or performing some service unasked, whether you wanted it or not, such as cleaning your already clean windscreen whenever your car was stopped at traffic lights.

Although it could be irritating, given some thought on the matter, one realised that these kids were only attempting to do their share of contributing to what almost certainly would be a very meagre family income.

Only in the villages was one able to come in contact with children in their natural habitat, and in every village I went to I found them laughing and friendly, and not in the least shy. I remember one occasion when I was visiting a village, with my wife, to see a sick child, when it suddenly started to rain. We took shelter in the doorway of the roofed village communal meetingplace, and suddenly heard children's voices singing what I presume was a children's song – like 'Hi ho, Hi ho,' of the dwarfs in the film *Snow White and the Seven Dwarfs*. As we peered out of the doorway a huge banana palm leaf came into view around the corner of our shelter, splattered on by the teeming rain, and with three small boys holding it up over their heads and marching along, one behind the other, completely dry, and singing their heads off.

Of all the countries in Africa, Ghana has a unique history that in times past greatly influenced the various tribes of which the nation was, and still is, composed, and that differentiates it from the rest of Africa, even to this day.

The Gold Coast, as Ghana and the surrounding area was called before it achieved Independence from Britain in 1957, was, from before the middle of the nineteenth century, one of the main places in Africa to which missionaries were sent from the United Kingdom, although there was a certain amount of overspill into what is now the Ivory Coast on the west, and Nigeria on the east (this last made famous as the area where the Dundee mill-girl, Mary Slessor, worked in Calabar).

Traditionally, many of these early missionaries died of malaria, yellow fever, and other tropical diseases, giving rise to that part of Africa becoming known as the White Man's Grave.

As a result of the concentrated missionary influence, however, Ghana is today a country with more churches, of every denomination imaginable, and more religious orders, than any other part of the world that I have had the opportunity to visit. All the Ghanaian friends I made were regular church-goers; but this seems to be part of their normal way of life, and little different than if they belonged to a bridge club in this much less religious country. Their religion was not a pious, `Holy Willie' type of faith, but was quite the reverse, and an opportunity I had of attending a church service, albeit on a rather special occasion, might offer an insight into church-going in Ghana – at least for some Ghanaians – compared to church-going in this country, wherever lessening church-going does still exist, in this less expressive society.

My quantity surveyor friend, Alex Kujiku, had been asked by the Minister of a church which lay to the north of Accra if he could help them with the construction of a small hall at the back of the church, and on its completion Alex had been invited to attend the Thanksgiving Service which was about to be held. He asked me if I would like to accompany him; so the two of us drove out in his car to the church, and on arriving were shown into a pew about the middle of the congregation.

There was no organ, but music for the hymns was supplied by a uniformed brass band which occupied a balcony behind the pulpit, and which was playing a selection of hymn music as we came in. The pews were by now quite packed, and people in different parts of the church were humming to the hymn tunes. When the music finally stopped, it took the Minister several minutes to get the congregation hushed for an opening prayer, and as he prayed, voices from different parts of the congregation said loud Amens.

Although this communal accompanying of the Minister's prayer was a matter of surprise to me, a dour Scottish Presbyterian, I could feel the genuine earnestness of the congregation, and in a curious way, and in that African church, and with the crowded exalting congregation, I felt a rapport that, when I thought back on it, quite astonished me.

Part way through the service there was a collection, which entailed the whole congregation filing, pew by pew, past a huge brass receptacle with a wide mouth into which each worshipper put his or her offering. When those in the pew in which we were sitting got up to join the long line of people waiting to make their offerings, Alex put his hand on my arm and signalled me to stay in my seat with him.

The procession of worshippers filing past the offering receptacle became a lane of singing, dancing, people, obviously generally experiencing a rapturous spiritual joy at this giving of their gifts to God, and I realised that for these people, whatever their beliefs, their faith was a reality to them in a way quite beyond my own comprehension, and I just marvelled at it.

While the collection was taking place the musicians in the balcony were playing what I presumed were hymn tunes, but tunes of a stirring nature with which I was unfamiliar, and as the procession of worshippers moved down the aisles towards the offering bowl – which twice, completely full, was replaced by an identical empty bowl – several of the worshippers made small dancing movements as they moved steadily forward.

One elderly lady, perhaps sixty, or even older (I find it difficult judging any lady's age), danced her way forward almost without stopping. And when I happened to mention this to someone in Accra later on, they laughed at my obvious astonishment at someone dancing in a church service, and said, 'Haven't you read in the Bible that "David danced before the Lord"?'

The return of Fabian Mork to Ghana in early 1995 marked the termination of the stream of volunteer plastic surgeons who, apart from developing the fledgling Reconstructive Plastic Surgery Unit, had so tactfully handled many of the problems inherent in pushing forward a new branch of surgery in a community which, while welcoming the advent of such an essential addition to Ghanaian surgery as a whole, faced many difficulties regarding the shortage of facilities already existing in Korle Bu Hospital.

From the medico-political point of view, the change-over to Ghanaian control of the Reconstructive Plastic Surgery Unit, and the cessation of the continuous stream of volunteer surgeons being responsible for the running of the Unit – and their part in the general function of Korle Bu Hospital – had a much more profound effect than at first might have been evident. It meant a diminution of the international support of the Project's aims for Ghana, and it meant a profound change in the attitude of the rest of Korle Bu staff's attitude to the Unit now that it was `one of them', and Mork had to battle for its development on equal terms with the rest of the Ghanaian surgical staff.

Professor Yeboah was an enormous help in dealing with these difficulties, but his astute promise of the inclusion of two leg-ulcer wards available to the whole surgical staff did a great deal to mollify all except a small hard core who, stirred up perhaps by one or two disgruntled individuals, were not happy with the developing situation and protested that with the Plastic Surgery addition, there were no empty beds available.

As a permanent member of staff, Fabian Mork was entitled to quarters adequate to accommodate his family, but the comfortable enough villa allotted to him was some considerable distance from the main hospital, where the Unit was situated, and he bought a rather aged car to get about in. From time to time his car would break down – almost fall to pieces might be a more correct term – and he had to call on the Unit's pick-up and driver to help him out, which in many instances produced no difficulty, but not always, as there sometimes was a clash between the need for the car for a visiting surgeon and for Mork's own use. But this was a minor problem which in no way overshadowed the immediate stabilizing effect which the long-awaited presence of Ghana's first trained plastic surgeon had on the staff of the Reconstructive Plastic Surgery Unit, who, despite the constant changing of surgeons-in-charge over a period of nearly three years, had kept together remarkably well.

Mrs Tay, with her remarkable organising ability, had arranged a welcome home party for Fabian, and had persuaded the Labadi Beach Hotel Management to house the celebrations and provide small snacks, without charge, while Ghana Brewery generously donated the drinks.

The Minister of Health officially welcomed Fabian and invited `The Father of the Project' to say a few words. In thanking the various people who had helped to make this new Branch of Surgery available to Ghana, I mentioned the tremendous burden that had been lifted from our shoulders by the donation of a room and breakfast – without charge – by Mr Molenschot of Shell Oil Company, and said I reckoned it saved us anything up to £15 per day. Whereupon Kees Molenschsot called out from the audience that it saved us much more than that as the £10 daily room cost for the Shell Company employees was heavily subsidised by the Company, so we were actually saving anything up to £25 a day. I apologised profusely for my error and vowed that even at £25 a day they were far superior rooms to any hotel I had stayed in – but the slight altercation took a little off the edge of the celebrations.

Mork settled in well despite his almost three years absence (as mentioned, once we were convinced of his trustworthiness, we had in fact allowed his family and children to come to Scotland on holiday), and gradually his own worth as a plastic surgeon began to convince those few who resented someone becoming a full member of the staff, with his own ready-made department, in this fashion. They were further mollified somewhat by the information that it had been decided by those running the Project – with Mork's full agreement – that, in view of the unusually complex surgical problems with which he was not yet familiar, a volunteer surgeon would continue to come out for a short period every three months to help him with these problems that he could not be expected to deal with without adequate experienced surgical back-up – as would be the case in any established Unit, such as Canniesburn Hospital, and which continues to be the case as far as Ghana is concerned, to this day.

This arrangement, while continuing to call on funds raised by the Project, works very well in practice, particularly as the three-monthly visit includes a short weekend trip by the visiting surgeon to Kumasi Hospital to help the surgeon there with some of their problem cases.

In the meantime, however, the news from Kumasi was not encouraging. When Pius Agbenorku had been taken on the staff of the

Komfo Anoyte Teaching Hospital as Consultant Plastic Surgeon in 1994, I had assumed he just had to get down to work and build up a small Reconstructive Plastic Surgery Unit. And we would help him from Accra as much as we could. It was six months later before I learned that he was working under extremely difficult circumstances, since, with the fourth theatre being out of action, there was no possibility that he could be given operating sessions in the other three very busy theatres – which no one seemed to have thought of when they appointed him.

His only opportunity of getting theatre facilities was in the Accident and Emergency Department, which had its own small theatre, and he had to slip his cases in whenever there was a lull in emergency surgery being carried out. This meant he might not get a chance to operate for a whole morning, and played havoc with giving premedication. To add to the difficulty, when there was no emergency surgery being carried out, the anaesthetist assigned to do duty in the A & E Department would frequently not be available, as he had to check on the condition of the patients who had been operated on earlier that day.

This was an almost intolerable situation, and the plastic surgery cases were regarded, with some justification, as a total nuisance by the staff of the A & E Department. Pius was apparently, and understandably, becoming totally disenchanted, and when I spoke to him on the phone I promised him I would do all I could to get the fourth unused theatre functioning somehow. The Kumasi surgical staff were full of encouragement, but I had no idea how I was going to keep my promise.

There were several equipment stores in Korle Bu Hospital, but none of them had anaesthetic machines, and purchasing one was quite out of the question. My driver told me, however, that he knew that there was a very large area equipment store in Tema about fifteen miles away, and I thought I might as well have a look at what it contained. To my surprise it had nine anaesthetic machines gathering dust, and waiting to be used when – and if – the surgical block in Korle Bu Hospital was ever restored to full working conditions. There were only eight theatres in the Korle Bu Hospital block so one of the machines must have been ordered as a spare, but work had not even begun in Korle Bu, and with the problems of funding a full reconstruction of the theatre block presently insoluble no one was going to miss the spare machine at all.

I went to see Commodore Obimpeh, the Minister of Health, in the hope that I could persuade him to release the extra anaesthetic machine, but to begin with he simply said I should take it up with the Chairman of the Hospital Management Board. I knew from previous experience, however, that at that level of authority no one would take the responsibility of releasing the extra machine.

As a politician, at first the Minister wasn't about to authorise an unofficial action for which he might be held responsible at a later date, but, faced with a situation where all of the nine machines might never be required – and possibly might not still be in good enough condition to function at all if things went on as they were doing, he finally gave me authority to uplift the spare machine – in our own transport – and not to start shouting about the matter all over the place.

The whole Kumasi surgical department was overjoyed at the news, for it would benefit everybody, not just Pius, and on the strength of it they persuaded some local sources to pay for air-conditioning to be installed in the long-unused fourth operating theatre. (And to think it had been really on a whim, not expecting anything to come out of it, that I had put my proposition to Obimpeh!)

Everything now seemed to be going to plan at last, and it was most rewarding when I was told that Pius had carried out his first full working operating session in the refurbished fourth theatre, and that the nine other sessions were a real godsend to the rest of the surgical staff. Another important advantage of Pius having his own fixed theatre sessions was that he could now make full use of the three-monthly visit of the volunteer surgeons to help with difficult operations, and he no longer needed to beg the use of a theatre and an anaesthetist for a special session when the visitors were due; which took place, if he was lucky, on a Saturday when the three other theatres were not normally being used, but which could not be banked on.

The Unit which Pius gradually built up was to receive a welcome boost in 1996 when Mr Arthur Morris, now an addition to the Project's Trustees, began to take a personal interest in it, with unforeseen achievements which are expanded on later in this narrative.

Meanwhile, following the enforced selection of architects who would build the new centre in Accra, a contract had been drawn up with a completion date in late 1996, but problems had arisen regarding finding a suitable site for the new building which, to avoid the high cost of installing elevators large enough to accommodate a bed and possibly attached apparatus, along with attendant staff, had been designed, apart from the Administrative Block, on one floor, considerably increasing the overall ground dimension.

There was plenty of land available in the extensive grounds of the hospital, but it was essential to have an active surgical unit, especially one dealing with serious burns, sited in the vicinity of the rest of the main hospital, with all the equipment and facilities to deal with any contingency which might arise, close to hand. Apart from this, it was essential to be within reach of the main electrical and other essential facilities, and in the end, a stretch of ground bordered closely on one side by the hospital staff tennis courts, and with hospital buildings nearby on two of the other sides, was selected; without detriment to the all-important tennis courts...

The foundation stone was duly laid on 20 March 1996 by Commodore Obimpeh, the Minister of Health, and building work proceeded from then on – albeit somewhat delayed.

The basic design of the building was in the form of an elongated H, with the main wards at the further end of the H, while the operating theatre block, with the recovery ward, formed the crossbar, and on the other side of this the two nearer parts of the H led into the two-storey, horizontally placed, administrative and general office area, with the lecture room and hospitality suite (for visiting surgeons) on the first floor.

This arrangement did mean quite a bit of leg-work getting from one end of the building to the other, but with no stairs in the main surgical part of the building the benefit of this, with so much movement of trolleys and beds, was readily appreciated, and as the building proceeded the uniqueness of the design, and the attractive frontage of the administrative block, convinced me – and others – of the rightness of sticking to Grüter's concept, despite the Hell and High Water it had occasioned, at least for me.

With Mork meantime making a very good job of developing the scattered unit in the main hospital, and with very much appreciation of the three-monthly appearance of the visiting surgeons allowing him to avoid undertaking potentially difficult problems single handedly, the reputation of the unit was increasing steadily, to the extent that the erstwhile grumblers amongst the surgical staff at the `intrusion' of this new branch of surgery had completely died down.

Professor Yeboah had continued to take a keen personal interest in the unit, making sure that the junior staff who worked with Mork were capable of keeping up with the running of the unit, but whenever possible, he chose juniors who might be interested in reparative surgery to the extent that they might eventually become fully-trained, and could help develop this specialised work in other areas of Ghana – part of the original aim of the Project's work.

One registrar in particular, Albert Paintsil, seemed ideally suited for this type of surgery, and was interested in taking it up as a career. He applied for training overseas and was ultimately accepted for training in the UK – indeed he was the last overseas trainee registrar to be accepted in the UK for the three-year course, as there were numbers of refugees and other incomers to Britain who were medically trained and hoped to specialise in plastic surgery if they were accepted into the registrar training scheme. We shall hear more of this young man in due course.

As the building, with innumerable delays, reached the stage of being roofed, and having the windows put in, a basic problem of the positioning of the building on a north–south axis – because of the shape of the ground available – became apparent, for as the overhead sun moved westward in the early afternoon, the scorching direct heat of its rays poured in increasingly through the windows, which had only small ventilators, and the heat trapped in the west-facing wards on that side became quite intolerable. The inevitable solution to the problem was to build adequate shading along the top of the window frames, but it added to the cost, and only partially resolved the difficulty.

Leaks in the roof, when heavy rains began, caused endless problems, as they seemed to continue to appear even after existing ones were repaired. To crown everything, woodworm began to affect the softwood surrounds of doors and windows and even some ceilings, requiring replacement of the untreated faulty softwood, or, where that would have been difficult, the faulty softwood having to be impregnated with special solutions, which are not always effective.

After much haranguing on the part of Mrs Tay – and myself when I was in Ghana – the problems, including some faulty plumbing which had led to burst pipes and floor flooding (even up to the week before the actual Opening Ceremony) were gradually overcome, and a new proposed opening date around the beginning of 1997 was suggested.

At the instigation of Dr Brookman-Amissah, the Minister of Health (Obimpeh to our great regret had moved to another Ministerial post), her deputy, Mr Nyama Donkor, came over daily to the building site with the intention of speeding up the work being carried out. While he is to be thanked for his efforts, there were still delays, with problems arising regarding the connection to the distant electric mains, and also with the water supply, so the early 1997 date was becoming doubtful. Of equal importance, at the rate things were proceeding, was the obvious impossibility of finishing the plastering and woodwork, not to mention laying the terrazzo flooring, in time, and it became apparent that the building would be nowhere near being ready to be opened at the beginning of the year as had been anticipated, and a new date of 26 May was decided on. The President, who had been formally invited to carry out the Opening Ceremony, was notified, and the State programme was duly altered.

What had not been revealed to us until now was that the work schedule had greatly failed to keep up with the programme to which the contractor was committed. The contractor's new assurance of the entire building being completed in time for the proposed new opening date gave me, and my advisers, considerable doubts about the building being completed by late May. The situation had called for a drastic rethink of the problems; and following that, it was decided to concentrate on the main part of the building; from the operating-theatre suite forward, and in particular the imposing two-storey administrative block and the wards between that and the theatre suite. Whilst a reduced amount of work continued in the two long blocks of wards on the far side of the operating-theatre/recovery room suite, the main efforts of the workmen were concentrated on the rest of the building, and the Presidential inspection tour would simply spend its time in that part of the building with the unfinished blocks closed off, an arrangement that actually worked perfectly on the actual day.

It now seemed that, despite the various setbacks, we could begin to contemplate the day when the Reconstructive Plastic Surgery Unit would at long last be transferred, lock, stock and barrel so to speak, to its custom-built new home, and I took up the matter of the increase in nursing staff which would be required, with the Hospital Administration. To my astonishment I was told that, while the nursing complement of nineteen at present staffing the RPS Unit would automatically be transferred to the new building when it was opened, with the acute shortage of nursing staff in the hospital as a whole no additional staff could be spared!

I couldn't believe what I was hearing, for we had worked out that once the new Centre was fully operational it would require sixty-eight nurses to cope with day and night shifts, nurses on leave and sick, and most importantly because the nurse-intensive Burns Wing would require double the number of nursing staff required in other wards. Added to this, we anticipated that when the Centre ultimately had its full complement of three surgeons, more staff would probably be required for the additional clinics that would likely be needed...

After all the effort that had been put in by so many individuals to achieve the final result we were anticipating, to learn that no provision was going to be made to provide enough nursing staff to enable what should have been a Centre of Excellence to function to its full capacity – or even half of that – was devastating.

I contacted the Ministry of Health, who said it was an internal hospital problem; and of course no one I approached in the Hospital Administration had any solution to offer.

As before, what I was afraid of was the possibility that, if the Centre was seriously under-used, it might be opened up to other branches of surgery, for there had already been unfavourable comments floating around that it was nonsense for a structure such as the Centre to be used only for one surgical specialty, when surgeons who had been on the Korle Bu staff for years were denied adequate bed space and facilities. No one mentioned the fact that we in the Project Charity had raised almost half a million pounds to help in its construction, and had been responsible for the entire equipping of the whole Centre.

If there were problems to be dealt with in Ghana, there was no lack of them back home in Scotland. To digress for a moment: before Fabian Mork had finished the training programme Martyn had set out for him, and returned to Ghana in mid-1995, I had brought the news to Glasgow of Rawling's `suggestion' that the Plastic Surgery Unit should be housed in a separate building of its own – and everyone thought that this was a marvellous idea. But when I went on to explain that the Project would have to take on the task of finding most of the funds to do so, it produced a very different reaction.

The concept of the dedicated building nevertheless gripped everyone I spoke to associated with the Ghana Project, and I got plenty of encouragement from my Scottish friends to `use my charm' and try to raise the money – in Ghana!

To be accurate, it must be mentioned that Rex Cook, the indomitable Helensburgh Rotarian, did actually raise funds from West of Scotland Rotarians, and it was one of these same Rotarians who had asked him the pertinent question – was the money they were donating just for the building, or did it include the furnishing and equipping, and the seventy-three beds? In the general confusion it had not occurred to anyone, including myself, that producing a bare building was only part of the problem!

By coincidence, shortly after it had been realised that the Project would be responsible for equipping the building, Rex was told by one of his fellow Rotarians that he had just been invited to collect five old hospital beds from a ward in the Glasgow Western Infirmary, part of which had closed down, and he understood that there were five other beds in the same ward looking for an owner. Rex, being Rex, got hold of the other five beds, although they were in rather poor condition, took them to pieces, put them in his garage, and told me about them. Following that, Martyn Webster and I began to look for similar disused beds in other closed-down places; and while we located some – regarding which we were told there was no hurry in removing them – the problem was where were we going to store them? And of course we still had no idea how we were going to get them out to Ghana.

The answer to the problem, when we finally came up with an answer, had its roots in an incident which had happened when I went out to Ghana to help Bainbridge get the Plastic Surgery Unit started up in

January 1993. While I was there Professor Yeboah honoured me by presenting me with a beautifully carved Chief's Stool (on which, as already explained, they sat when in tribal conference), and had my name engraved on the side of it. These stools were carved from a single piece of hardwood and were so heavy it was extremely difficult for me to lift, and it was obvious that I could not take it home by air. I happened to mention the matter to an English friend I had made in Accra, Tom Cregg, the MD of Ghana Bauxite, who said that one of the ships that his Company chartered to take the bauxite ore back to the parent Company in Burntisland, on the Firth of Forth in Scotland, could take it back without any difficulty provided I had it wrapped up securely. But I had forgotten all about this two years later when we were discussing the matter of equipping the proposed new Reconstructive Plastic Surgery building.

By December of that year I was due to go back again to Ghana, and my wife, Maisie, was coming out with me on this, her first visit to the country. She found the heat very difficult to deal with, but despite that she was intrigued with the city of Accra, and most impressed with the Shell Guest House – although I had to leave her on her own there quite a lot of the time whilst I was making cap-in-hand calls, and going over to see how the Unit in Korle Bu Hospital was progressing under Bainbridge.

Although when I first began going out to Ghana I had received a few invitations to dinner from my Ghanaian and British friends, over the course of time, with three-monthly visits to Ghana these invitations had gradually become fewer, but on the occasion when my wife came out with me we received an invitation to a supper party at the Yeboahs' home.

They lived some distance out of Accra, in the direction of Tema, beside a small village called Teshi; and the invitation said 6.30 p.m. As there was a well-known Fine Art Centre, with paintings and sculptures by well-known Ghanaian artists, on the main road near Teshi I thought it would be interesting to both of us to stop and have a look at it on our way to the Yeboahs.

Maisie, a stickler for being on time, felt we should leave the hotel about half past five but I explained that Ghana time was more relaxed than British time and six o'clock would be early enough. We left at half past five. As we neared the Art Centre I suddenly saw a rather unusual display in a shop with a large glass front and told the driver to stop and reverse a short distance so that we could have a proper look at the curious objects I thought I had seen. When I could properly see what was in the window I got out to have a closer look, as I just could not believe my eyes. I was looking into a showroom with really large models of cars, planes, ships, even a railway engine; and animals – elephants, camels, ostriches and other curious creatures, all in most striking eye-catching colours. But each of them was built around a standard wooden coffin!

Noticing a door on the side of the building I walked over to have a peek inside, and found I was obviously looking into the workshop where all these extraordinary articles were made. One of the men, busy carving a wooden lion's head with a mallet and chisel, came over and explained there was quite a demand for these bizarre coffins, but mostly in other parts of the country, and he believed that his was the only place in Ghana where they were made. I had seen in many countries, particularly in South America, undertaker's shops on roads leading up to hospitals with coffins openly displayed around the entrance, but nothing like this.

By now the driver had appeared at the door to say my wife was getting rather worked up at the delay, and when I got back to the car she said we had no time now to see the Art Centre, which she had particularly wanted to visit, and no suggestion from me that on `Ghana time' we were not going to be all that late made any difference.

We arrived at the Yeboahs' at about five past seven and stood for a moment at the gate to see if anyone else might be going in. As there was no one else in sight we walked in and could see a number of tables set out in the garden, with plates and cutlery, and with a large unlit candle in the centre of each table – and through the open kitchen door we could see Margaret, Eddie's wife, and some helpers, busy preparing dishes of appetizing foodstuffs. After a moment, Eddie himself appeared, pulling on his jacket. He was obviously slightly disturbed to find us there, and glancing at his wrist watch, said, `You're a bit early: but take a seat – anywhere you like – and I'll get you a drink.'

It was about eight o' clock before the first of the other guests began to arrive, and by now all the candles were lit. So Maisie learned the hard way the real difference between `Ghana time' and `British time'.

The highlight of our three weeks stay was to be a four-day trip we were going to make, as Christmas guests of Tom and Mavis Cregg, up into the coolness of the high mountains some fifty miles north of Kumasi. Tom was, as I said, the Managing Director of the Ghana Bauxite Company, and apparently the high hills were practically made of bauxite. He and his wife spent part of their time in Accra and part of their time in the coolness of their hill station, where they kept a couple of horses and had a magnificent swimming pool, and we were looking forward to this break tremendously.

Tom had a very good relationship with his staff, who had, by themselves, organised a singalong on Christmas Eve, which we all joined in – aided by a Scotch or two – and I have never seen a Boss so well liked by his staff.

During our very enjoyable weekend with them, Tom asked me about the rumours he had heard that we were building a Centre solely for plastic surgery and burns. I told him how things stood, and suddenly saw a ray of hope for solving the problem of sending out the beds which we were intending to collect. There was no problem, he said, as the specially constructed ore ships were often more or less empty on the UK–Ghana trip, and he told me to contact Mr Dougan, the Financial Director of Alcan Chemicals Europe, in Burntisland, about it when I got back to Scotland.

By the time I did get back home to Ayr, I found the word about our endeavours to collect beds – and, hopefully, equipment – for Ghana had spread, and it had come to the ears of Mr Douglas Brown, formerly Surgeon in Charge of the Orthopaedic wards, and now the Chairman of the South Ayrshire Hospital NHS Trust, who asked me to come and see him regarding the problem. We were old colleagues, and after I had given him a condensed account of the Ghana situation he told me that the Plastic Surgery wards and operating theatres in Ballochmyle Hospital, some twelve miles away, had been closed down for in-patient work some years after the Central Plastic Surgery Unit in Canniesburn Hospital in Glasgow had opened up in 1968. He said the Unit in Ballochmyle Hospital was completely furnished and equipped, and in very good condition, despite the length of time it had remained mothballed and unused, and with most of the hospital in Ballochmyle now closed he saw no reason why we should not be able to take whatever we wished for the Unit in Ghana.

A few weeks later he informed me that the local Hospital Board would be prepared to let us have any of the equipment, beds and furnishing from the old Plastic Surgery Unit that we could use in Ghana, but that we must move everything out by our own efforts. I contacted one of the largest removal firms in Scotland, John Russell & Co, which I knew had huge storage areas in Glasgow, and it appeared that one of the sons, Kenneth Russell, had his own Company, Deanside Transit, within the main yard. I went to see him personally, and he was most interested in what we were doing for Ghana. To cut a long story short, in due course, without charge, six forty-foot containers were sent down to uplift all we had selected, and with the very active help of those porters still employed in Ballochmyle Hospital (whose enthusiastic services are recognised on plaques fixed on the wall above two beds in one of the wards in the new Centre), everything we had collected was packed, with some difficulty, into the six containers.

This practice of attracting donations, in kind or in cash, by fixing a named plaque on the wall above a cot, a bed or at the door of a special room, or a ward, or a whole Wing – depending on the amount donated – was started shortly after the building work had commenced, and culminated with the gifting by the Japanese Government, through their Contingency Funds, of the cost of the whole multi-roomed, twin operating theatre suite and recovery area – almost a third of the cost of the building itself – to commemorate which a large plaque was fixed alongside the theatre suite entrance. The invaluable help given to us by Deanside Transit and Alcan Chemicals in moving all the goods we had gathered to furnish and equip the Centre, was likewise acknowledged.

To return to the matter of the equipment we had collected from Ballochmyle Hospital: Mr Russell arranged for everything to be put into a large locked shed until we were able to identify suitable locked accommodation in Korle Bu Hospital in Ghana. This last proved a considerable problem, but with the aid of a little `encouragement', space enough was eventually identified and cleared of whatever had originally been in it.

After Customs Clearance Certificates had been obtained, and suitable sailing dates arranged, Deanside Transit reloaded the six containers and transferred them to Burntisland for shipment in one of the ore ships shortly due to leave Alcan Chemicals Europe's dock en route to Ghana At the Ghana end, Korle Bu Hospital had kindly agreed to arrange for contractors to move the containers, once cleared by the Customs – which took long and lengthy discussions, examinations, and downright arguments – to the hospital, have them emptied, and transferred back to the docks at Tema, from where they were eventually shipped back to Burntisland, and finally on to Glasgow.

Despite the less than gentle handling, the condition of the equipment, the theatre lamps, the operating tables, the beds, lockers, suction machines, anaesthetic machines, and indeed everything we took to Ghana, was extremely good, although by no means new. And it meant that the Reconstructive Plastic Surgery and Burns Centre in Korle Bu Hospital would be able to start up, after the Official Opening Day, fully equipped, and including everything that we could have wished for in a modern well-run specialty centre anywhere. Except for the very real problem of not having enough nurses to run it properly.

(Now that it is all over and everything is safely installed in the new Centre in Ghana – and also that Mr Brown is retired and Ballochmyle Hospital has been totally demolished – it has to be confessed that if a particularly useful anaesthetic machine or other piece of apparatus – or furniture – happened to find its way down the corridor to the plastic surgery wards when we were clearing them out, no one was about to stop it.)

On top of the problems arising regarding the building of the Centre, problems had arisen regarding our accommodation; for the Shell Oil Company had notified us in early 1996 that they intended selling the Guest House and regretted they would no longer be able to help us with accommodation. This was a considerable shock, as it left us with the very real problem of not having anywhere similar, at the reduced cost Shell had favoured us with all that time, and would need to look around elsewhere for modestly priced accommodation for future Project volunteers; and the room cost at least would have to be met by the Project's funds.

A number of the less expensive hotels were looked at, as was the Guest House of the Volta River Association, where I stayed for two nights, when by chance I happened to run into Bernard Antoine, the Managing Director of the Novotel, which was in the centre of town. As recounted earlier, I had stayed at the hotel as a guest a couple of years before, and had got on very well with Bernard and his wife Jennie; and I had made a practice subsequently of taking friends to dinner there whenever the occasion arose. Bernard already knew about the Shell Guest House closing, and asked me what we were going to do. I told him the matter was still not decided, and was proving very much of a problem. He said he and Jennie greatly admired what we were doing for Ghana, and that he would be happy to allow a substantial discount for any of the volunteers staying at the Novotel: an offer I gratefully accepted and which was much appreciated. When I came out again to Ghana some two months later, I stayed there myself, and he insisted that I was his personal guest – a wonderful help for the Project budget – and knowing that his taste in Scotch whisky coincided with mine, I had brought him a duty-free litre of Macallan, a token of my appreciation of his kindness, a custom I kept up as long as I continued to go out to Ghana.

As the date for the opening of the Centre drew near it had been decided by the Project Trustees that those in Scotland who had been most involved with the Project – doctors, nurses and others – should be invited to come out, with spouses, on ten-day excursion fares; and on the Saturday before the Opening on the following Thursday 26 May a party of twenty-two people travelled out together, including the only non-Scot, Jackie Fairweather, a British Airways hostess from the south of England, who had come to know the Project volunteers personally as they passed through Gatwick Airport on the way to Ghana, and who brought out a huge quantity of toys donated by herself and all her colleagues, for the children – of which more later.

The Novotel Management had arranged a generous discount for the visitors (with my wife and me having a suite to ourselves as Bernard's guests!) and to crown everything, they threw a magnificent moonlight buffet-supper beside the pool to climax the actual opening day.

We had arrived on the Saturday evening, as planned, and the following morning I took my son David with me to see how matters were progressing at the Centre. As we drove up to the front of the building we were appalled at the muddy state of the ground, and realised that after two nights' tropical rain, the contractor's heavy lorry traffic had reduced the whole area in front of the building to a quagmire, making it almost impossible to approach the entrance; we were well over our shoes in mud by the time we had reached it.

The sight that met us when we went into the building really chilled us, for many of the walls had still to be plastered, and terrazzo flooring had not even been laid in several areas – and it was obviously quite impossible for the opening to take place on the Thursday. But what completely stunned us, more than the unfinished building, was the huge piles of litter and rubbish lying everywhere, half filling many of the rooms – and when we removed some of it, areas of unfinished skirting, and even flooring, were revealed.

As it happened, the Chief of Protocol, the individual responsible for the President's safety, and thus responsible for seeing that everything was in order for His Excellency's visit to open the Centre – and nobody, but nobody, could contradict the Chief of Protocol – arrived shortly after us; and without even going beyond the Administration block he declared, rather tersely, that he could not possibly allow the President to open the Centre on the Thursday – and probably not for some considerable time after that.

CHAPTER 5

David and I were shattered at what the Chief of Protocol had said, although as things stood, it was obvious that he was right. David spoke with him about the possibility of getting extra labourers – at his expense, and offering incentives to the existing working party to speed things up.

`This is not Scotland, you know!' the Chief said, `and speeding up workers is not a phrase you could translate to these people, who are no better and no worse than any other workers in Ghana.'

David explained about the enormous amount of undisposed rubbish lying everywhere, and the appearance of chaos which it gave, while the actual state of the building work was not as bad as the uncollected rubbish made it appear. He pleaded with the Chief to be given the chance at least to try to get it completed in time, no matter how much it cost him.

The Chief could see the distress on David's face, and he knew the bitter disappointment a postponement would mean for the visitors from Scotland who had each done so much to make it possible for Ghana to have a Reconstructive Plastic Surgery Service at all. And after a lengthy discussion of what David might be able to achieve, with extra help, it was agreed that, if by midday on Thursday the Centre, apart from the two quite extensive furthest away blocks of wards – which would be closed off – had the appearance of being completed, he would allow the President to perform the Opening Ceremony on Friday 27 June – one day late.

For the rest of the Sunday, David went round every room and corridor area, making a note of what was still required to be done, and by which workers, and he pinned a copy of these instructions at the entrance to every room or passageway so that the men could refer to it and get on with whatever work they could with as little confusion as possible, whether they were plasters, painters or carpenters.

An experienced businessman, David had an almost uncanny knack of handling workmen, or those employed by him – a mixture of friendliness and discipline. Everyone had to be on first name terms – including himself (probably the first time most of the workmen had addressed a white man by his first name), and yet without any argument he fired two of the workmen he discovered asleep during their night shift.

On the Monday morning at 7 a.m. be explained the situation to the workforce and offered double pay for those who would work in shifts through the night, in addition to a bonus for everybody if the Thursday target was met.

After he told them about the notices at each doorway, and how the men should get on with their own different jobs wherever they found their services could be used, he had the whole group clearing away and burning or burying all of the rubbish lying around; and after that they got on with their different tasks with quite remarkable effectiveness.

David hardly slept at all during these three-and-a-half days and nights, but he had the men laughing and joking with him – and he got the work done.

The muddy ground outside was at first a great problem as the lorries had churned it up really badly. Luckily the rain had stopped during the previous night, and the ground was drying quickly, so David paid for five huge lorryloads of pebble gravel to be distributed over the smoothed-out ground to a depth of almost three inches, and it made an almost perfect walking surface on the actual Opening Day.

While all this work was going on, Mrs Tay, along with Professor Yeboah, had arranged daily minibus tours for the rest of the group, with a very active programme of visits to various parts of the city, and an outdoor luncheon at a famous School of African Dancing some five miles west of the city and right on the cliff top above the Atlantic ocean.

There were visits to the large marketplace in Accra, which was listed in a brochure as the Art Centre, and certainly Ghanaian Art in the form of elaborate carvings in hardwood, some of which were really exquisite, could definitely come under the heading of Art.

One special visit was a whole day trip to see the enormous Volta Dam, which had been built some twenty years or so ago to provide generator power, mainly to serve the large aluminium smelting works and other industrial plants close to Tema, the country's biggest deep-water port. Electric power for the cities and towns was also dependant on the Volta generators.

The drive to the dam was along a highway running through an attractive valley which wound its way in and out of a ridge of low hills, and finally emerged on to the flatter ground that ran towards Akosombo, a small town that lay some three miles above the dam itself. Driving along the gradually climbing highway, rounding a sharp bend in the road suddenly brought the whole panorama of the huge dam into view, stretching across the entire skyline in front of the minibus. As they drew nearer to the dam the visitors' attention was drawn to a huge metal bridge, arching high into the air as it crossed the Volta river running tumbling towards the sea. At the far end of the bridge, and about half way up the hillside, stood a magnificent building – reminiscent of the one, lower down the river, where President Rawlings had authorised the Project to go ahead with its suggestion regarding bringing

Reconstructive Plastic Surgery to Ghana, and another extravagance of Nkruma, Ghana's first President, which contrasted with the poverty of the nearby countryside.

A little further downstream there was a much smaller public bridge over which ran a branch of the main road, giving access to the land on the far side of the waters above the dam.

Rounding a further bend in the main road, and having started to climb a branch road going to the right, the bus party was suddenly confronted with the full splendour of the Akosombo Hotel, perched on a small plateau overlooking the whole vista of the Akosombo dam.

Owned by the same firm as the Novotel in Accra, the hotel was positioned in such a way that the view from the balcony, which ran along the full length of the hotel, provided a breath-catching vista of the wide valley lying below the towering dam, the full length of which, filling the whole horizon, seemed to reach right up into the sky, and provided a fitting background to the deep valley which the hotel overlooked, with the huge jets of water shooting out from the generator exits along the face of the dam and crashing down onto the tangle of enormous rocks below. The balcony seemed almost directly above all this turbulent rushing water, but it must have been half a mile away at the very least.

After a splendid lunch on the balcony, the journey back took a different route and went through the moderately hilly country one could see looking north from Accra. Having passed through the town of Aburi, they were just about to begin the winding descent to the distant plains when the minibus came to a sudden halt, and then started to back towards a set of splendid ironwork gates they had just passed. The driver apologised, and said he was day dreaming and had clean forgotten to stop at the National Botanic Gardens – a must for any visitor to this part of Ghana.

Passing on foot through the tall, beautifully wrought double gates, the splendour of the Gardens was immediately apparent, for it contained magnificent specimens of all the trees and plants that were native to Ghana, and in the centre of the extensive gardens stood an enormous cottonwood tree, said to be the largest in the whole of Ghana. Cottonwood trees can reach enormous dimensions, and some of the older ones in the park apparently rivalled the American redwoods in height. Like them the trunk was totally bare of branches, with the foliage at the very top.

Not being conifers they have a totally different leaf structure from redwoods and when the tree fruits it produces myriads of small seed pods which, on ripening, burst open to emit a long white, cotton-like thread, several yards in length, with the aid of which they can be carried on the wind for long distances away from the tree. Thousands of white silky threads lay on the vegetation everywhere around, and produced an effect like snow surrounding the tree, extending a hundred yards or more in every direction.

This apart, the feature of the huge tree that had the most striking effect was the huge ridges, some fifteen feet in height, which projected further and further away from the trunk of the tree as they ran down and in to the ground. These, it turned out, were the roots of the tree, and reaching out ten feet or more as they disappeared into the ground, would obviously provide the permanent stability such a tall tree would require. The cottonwood trees, and the closely forested park itself with the numerous birds fluttering in the tree tops, gave one a feeling of being in the original jungle.

As we walked towards the gateway on our way out, we noticed, on one side of the main entrance pathway, a grove of trees which had been planted by eminent visitors over the years, and bronze plaques fixed to the tree trunks bore, amongst others, the names of several members of the British Royal Family, one of the largest trees having been planted by Prince Philip, the Duke of Edinburgh.

When the Head of Protocol arrived at the Centre on Thursday, he could scarcely believe his eyes, and as he walked through those parts of the building the President would actually see, he kept saying, `I really can't believe it is the same place!' At the end of his tour he agreed that the Opening Ceremony would take place the following day, with the President arriving at 11 a.m. He also managed to have the information broadcast on the TV and inserted in the evening papers, and explained the change of day to the President's involvement in negotiations regarding the threatening war situation in Sierra Leone.

There was a problem, however, for although we had persuaded the contractor to fix the operating theatre lamp on the ceiling in the theatre nearest completion (the other we simply shut off), all of the rest of the equipment, including the beds, bedside cabinets, and all other furnishings, was still in the locked hospital store where it had been lying, gathering dust, since it had arrived in Ghana some months before.

There was no question of moving it all up to the now empty Centre, but we had to make some sort of show of furnishing and equipping at least those wards and rooms through which we intended to take the President, and other visitors, after the actual Opening Ceremony. The hospital put three large vans at our disposal, and with the help of almost all of the plastic surgery staff, and as many patients as we deemed fit enough, we got to work, as soon as the Chief of Protocol had given the all clear, transferring what we reckoned would be essential.

By late evening we had everything installed, including the operating table and imposing-looking equipment in the one completed theatre where the theatre lamp had been fixed already. (As a matter of interest, when Rawlings was shown into the theatre, he actually did put his hand up to the large central theatre lamp, and moved it to see that it worked!)

On the morning of Friday 27 May the twenty-two of us arrived about half past nine at the immaculate-looking Centre, on which David had worked so hard to make an Opening Day possible, to find that, overnight, contractors had erected open-sided coloured pavilions to shelter spectators from the heat of the sun. There were three of them, forming the sides of a square facing the raised dais, with its own protecting pavilion for the officials accompanying the President and me – and with no rain overnight the gravel-covered ground formed a perfectly firm surface for people to walk on, with not a speck of mud in sight. The two pavilions at either side of the square were quite extensive, for these were to shelter the staff and their families and friends, while the one facing the dais was smaller and was for the `Scottish Party', and behind them, Senior Administrative and Government staff and their families and friends. These important guests all had individual chairs, while the occupants of the two larger pavilions had extensive seating provided in the form of long wooden benches – but most people had brought a cushion with them to sit on.

The dais party – the Minister of Health, Mrs Mary Grant, and the various Ambassadors and others who had helped directly with the building, including Mr Ian Mackley, who was the British High Commissioner at that time – were all seated at 10.30 a.m. in very comfortable chairs on the dais itself awaiting the arrival of the President. There had been some anxiety that morning when, true to form, fate had stepped in with the declaration of a State of War in Sierra Leone; and with Ghana being heavily involved militarily, there was considerable uncertainty as mobile phone messages came through, as to whether Rawlings might be tied up in the matter and at the last moment have to send someone else to carry out the Opening Ceremony.

Ultimately the British High Commissioner, who had his own mobile with him and was in constant touch with his deputy, who was in The Castle reporting the progress of the Council of War, told us they were on the way, and shortly after 11 o'clock we heard the noise of police whistles coming towards the hospital, and a few minutes later the whole Presidential entourage swept into the area where we were standing waiting for him and the cheering began – louder perhaps than it might have been if we hadn't had this scare that Rawlings might at the last moment be unable to attend, but everyone rose to their feet and gave vent to their feelings of relief with a resounding roar.

We had brought over a piper from Scotland with us, and playing `The Flowers of Scotland' he marched with great ceremony in front of the President as he and I made our way to the sheltered dais.

The sun was now at its highest, and all of those who had been waiting so long were beginning to find the heat almost unbearable. Fortunately, caterers had been hired to bring cooling drinks to those in the central VIP pavilion and on the dais, and I could see thermos flasks being passed round amongst the occupants of the two other pavilions.

When the President and I had taken our seats, the Chief of Protocol made the formal announcement 'The President of the Republic of Ghana,' and Rawlings walked forward to the podium, with a military guard standing close behind him.

He extolled what the Project had done for Ghana, and stated that, with this Reconstructive Plastic Surgery and Burns Centre that he was about to open, Ghana would stand head and shoulders above all other sub-Saharan countries in respect of the facilities and expertise that Ghana now possessed in this field.

As he invariably did when making a formal speech, he ended up by diverting from his official remarks and began talking off the cuff of his deep concerns regarding the disgraceful situation created by the International Monetary Fund in order to ensure repayment of the interest on the debt Ghana owed, with all medicines, medical advice, and medical or surgical treatment, having to be paid for – there was no free medicine – and it meant the poorest people could not afford any treatment whether surgical or medical.

He waved his hand over the British contingent and said, `I am asking you people to set up a Fund to help the poorer people in Ghana pay for their treatment in your new Centre.'

Following the main speeches, the Protocol Officer came over and asked me, along with Mrs Tay, to sit on a bench along with three other Europeans we had not met before.

The President then faced the crowd of onlookers, and one of his officials announced that President Rawlings was going to show Ghana's gratitude to the five of us for what we had done for his country by awarding us Membership of the Order of the Volta, the highest honour Ghana could bestow. Mrs Tay and the three people we did not know but who had been involved in humanitarian work in the North, were presented with medals of the first rank, which were duly pinned on them, and I was astounded to be bedecked with a sash supporting a very large medallion, creating me an Officer of the Volta – the equivalent of a Knight of the Order.

After this, wearing our medals – and me with my sash – we trooped over to the entrance of the Centre where, when I offered the Ceremonial Scissors to the President to cut the tape, he insisted that I should do this myself. We then made a tour of the main part of the Centre, including the wards that were open, and no one seemed to notice that we passed quite a few closed doors as we went round...

After the opening I had the honour of introducing the other members of our Scottish contingent to the President; and when he came to David (I had told him briefly, when we were sitting together on the dias, what my son had done) as he shook David's hand vigorously, he said `A chip off the old block, I can see...'

Having gone over to speak to the Nursing Stall, Rawlings asked to meet the piper; and nothing would have it but, having shaken the man's hand, he took the pipes into his own hands and played a few strangled notes, to the delight of the crowds gathered round.

On a continuing lighter note, once the President had left, some of the Scottish 'Party', before returning for a late lunch at the hotel, had gone across to the wards in the Children's Block where babies and small children under Fabian's care were all looked after in one ward, so that Jackie Fairweather could distribute the toys she had brought out to give to the children. The smallest patients were in cots with let-down sides, and when she came to one which held a little girl who had scars on her face and arms, Jackie selected a big white woolly rabbit, but when she attempted to give it to the child the little girl shrank away screaming, and in floods of tears.

Jackie was understandably shocked, until the Ward Sister explained that the child had had severe burns, requiring weeks of changing of dressings, and she obviously thought the white object was more painful dressings! A blue-dressed, pink-faced dolly was eagerly accepted, and the screaming and the crying stopped instantly as the child clutched the dolly close to her scarred cheek. By the time we had moved over to the cots on the other side of the ward we could hear the erstwhile terrified child speaking what we assumed was African baby-language to what was probably the first real toy she had ever had.

As mentioned earlier, the Novotel Hotel had laid on a magnificent buffet supper in the cool of the evening beside the swimming pool, and this rounded off a most memorable day in grand style.

And for one who knew the background to the possible scenario that might have wrecked the whole Opening Day episode, it meant I could have the first good night's sleep I had had since arriving, just a week before, in Ghana, a name now burned on my heart with a red hot poker.

The Saturday after the Opening was spent by most of the visiting party making last minute purchases, but as David had missed out on seeing anything of Ghana because of his determination to meet the Chief of Protocol's deadline, Alex Kujikn insisted on taking David and me on a rapid sight-seeing tour of the Dam at Akosombo, and the Botanic Park at Aburi. When the time came, we actually did them in the reverse order, and on the way back were fortunate to find the whole chimpanzee tribe crossing the road, with the younger ones chasing each other and having mock fights, with screaming and baring of teeth, but no actual injuries as far as one could tell.

On Sunday, prior to our return home overnight, we were paid the signal honour of being invited to attend a Durbar – an Indian term meaning `A Reception at the Court of a Native Ruler', as the Principal Guests of the Paramount Chief Djan Kwase II, Head of the Aknopen Tribe.

A Paramount Chief is next in rank to a king, and the Durbar was an acknowledgment of what the Project was doing for the Ghanaian people. It was an unexpected, but most appreciated, indication that the Ghanaian people were aware of the benefits that the Project was seeking to bring to them.

The Durbar was to be held on the gently sloping side of a hill covered in grass, which was part of a property owned by an English lady who had been of great help in designing and cultivating a Japanese garden beside the new Centre – to honour the Japanese for their generous contributions, and help in making it possible for the Centre to exist at all.

Arriving shortly before noon, in glorious sunshine, we found our hostess had set out a light buffet under a large awning. We could see the site for the Durbar on the sloping ground above, and were able to make out a large semi-circle of chairs.

The mountains rising steeply on either side added to the majesty of the scene, and created a natural amphitheatre covered in green grass on our hostess's property; conveying the impression of a stage waiting for the actors to appear.

We were ushered up towards the semi-circle of chairs, and my wife and I were invited to sit on the chairs next to a small gap, with Douglas Brown and his wife next to us, then Martyn Webster and his wife, with the rest of the party seated on the remaining chairs of the semi-circle. From our slightly elevated position we had a glorious view right down the valley, with the beautiful colours of the trees beyond. We were all commenting on the scene when we suddenly heard the noise of a drum-beat behind us, and almost immediately the figure of our host, the Paramount Chief, appeared, resplendent in his very colourful robes of Ghanaian woven cloth with a rich gold and black check, and wearing a gold crown. He was carrying a very ornate staff, marvellously decorated in gold, and wearing luxuriously decorated open-toed sandals.

Tribesmen carrying very colourful parasols were protecting the Chief and the high ranking tribesmen from the sun as this most colourful procession made its way towards the chairs to the right of me, just beyond the small gap in the semi-circle.

As the Paramount Chief moved forward, to the constant beating of the drums, he was followed by his large retinue of Office Bearers, each carrying his staff of office surmounted by a golden emblem denoting his badge of authority, and I was reminded of the procession of Chiefs at the funeral Service I had attended with Alex Kujiku, but the magnificence of the Paramount Chief's retinue was considerably beyond anything I had seen on that occasion.

The chairs on the other side of the gap from us were gradually filled by the Chief and his splendidly costumed followers, everyone carefully keeping to his station according to his rank.

When the main procession had entered the 'Arena', the Paramount Chief's First Wife, followed by his other three wives accompanied by their ladies-in-waiting, took their seats, with the First Wife sitting on the first row of seats alongside the Paramount Chief; and the other wives, resplendent in their very colourful costumes, sitting, with their ladies-in-waiting, in a row directly behind. The whole of the Royal Party formed a very cheerful, if noisy, group of people, and they were, like us, fully enjoying the occasion.

Once everyone was seated, six tribesmen came into the semi-circle and poured from a dark green bottle a liquid (which we were told was gin!) onto the ground before them, and danced and sang to banish any evil spirits(!) that may have been around.

At a signal, the drum-beating stopped, and the Paramount Chief rose to his feet, turned towards his guests, and in his own language bade us welcome, and expressed the gratitude and thanks of all his people for the benefits we had brought to Ghana. On receiving a signal, I rose, and in my own language, thanked him for his gracious remarks. Drum-beating started up once more, and we were entertained by the tribesmen dancing, followed by the wives who invited us to dance with them. It was all very entertaining; they held what looked like a dishcloth in their hands and waved it about furiously, so we brought out our handker-chiefs and did the same.

Following this the Chief rose to his feet and I was asked to go forward and stand in front of him, along with my wife. He was holding a large, beautifully executed mahogany carving, and I listened intently to what he had to say, although I could only guess what he was actually saying, but I gathered that he was presenting the carving to me as a thank you gift. Once he had finished we were guided back to our chairs, and the carving was later taken down to the minibus – to finally be presented to the Alloway Parish Church which had done so much to help us in our work in Ghana. When Maisie and I had returned to our seats, Douglas Brown and his wife were then presented with an equally large carving, with the same degree of ceremony. (He later presented his to the Hospital in Ayr.)

The drum-beating started up again, and we were further entertained with dancing by a number of the Chief's retinue in energetic African fashion, which exhibits exuberance as well as skill. Suddenly the Chief himself leaped to his feet and began to dance – and as he moved gradually towards our group the other dancers moved away, so that eventually the Chief came right up in front of me, gyrating and leaping. Suddenly everyone from his entourage, both men and women, rose to their feet and clapped their hands in time to the rhythm of the drums. One of the attendants whispered in my ear that the Chief's dance was a special mark of his appreciation to me personally – and was entirely spontaneous since the Chief had never been seen dancing since he was crowned, twenty-five years ago.

This performance brought the whole fascinating afternoon to an end, and when the Chief and his retinue retired the way they had entered, to drum-beating music, some of his lesser tribesmen stayed behind and spoke with us about what had taken place this afternoon.

Totally separate from the Durbah proceedings, in a lower part of our hostess's grounds, there was a turret-like building, somewhat similar to a bandstand, and local children, hearing the drum-beating, had found their way to where the Durbar was being held, and climbed up on to the peculiar structure to get a better view. When the Durbah had ended, my son David, a father himself, wandered over to see what the yelling and laughing kids were up to and found there were children of all ages, from toddlers eighteen to twenty months old to bigger children of possibly twelve or thirteen years, playing about on the building. He had his Compact Digital Viewcam with him and he started photographing the kids having fun. When some of them saw themselves on the rerun screen they were totally mesmerised, and there were shrieks of laughter as the older ones pulled funny faces and then howled with glee as they saw themselves on the little screen.

We collected some money from our group and gave it to the children to share out for sweets. They were delighted, and by the time the minibus arrived to take us back, the children had already run off – presumably to spend the small sum we had collected for them. We were particularly pleased to see the minibus arrive, for several of the adult tribesmen who had waited behind had been pestering David to film them also and run the pictures back. With difficulty we rescued him from the crowd that was besieging him, and, having thanked our hostess most warmly for her hospitality and kindness, we finally made our way back to the Novotel, very happy indeed, to prepare for our departure home later in the evening.

With the Opening Ceremony safely over, the transfer of the Reconstructive Plastic Surgery Unit from the surgical block to its own premises in the new Reconstructive Plastic Surgery and Burns Centre (RPS & B Centre) had to be organised. Basically, apart from the nursing staff and the patients, still spread in ones and twos in different wards in the surgical block, there was also a considerable amount of equipment belonging to the Unit, partly in some of the wards and partly in the Children's Operating Theatre, which the surgeons in the Unit had latterly used; but more particularly in Fabian's office which, over the course of time, had become a secure store for instruments and equipment that were not going to be used until the Unit moved over into its new quarters.

The Administrative area in the Centre was itself more or less complete, so that the surgeons' offices, and that of Mrs Oppong, our first Matron, could be occupied right away, and clinics could be held. By waiting for a few weeks before the main transfer took place, however, the contractor was able to finish off all the building work that had still to be done in the wards and in the operating-theatre suite. (The blocked off wards in the part of the Centre beyond the operating-theatre suite would take another six months before they were able to be used.)

With all the additional ward space that would be becoming available it was obvious that there was going to be a severe shortage of nursing staff; at that particular time there were only nineteen nurses out of a total complement of sixty-eight which would be needed to run the whole seventy-three bed Centre effectively, and efforts would have to be made to obtain as many new nurses as quickly as possible, a problem that was to bedevil the work of the Centre in the immediate future. Ironically, it was perhaps just as well, therefore, that not all of the Centre was yet complete.

The fact that neither of the operating theatres was yet in commission because there were problems with the condensers – integral parts of the air-conditioning system – meant that while the patients could be accommodated in the Centre, any operations that were required still entailed the patient, on a theatre trolley, being transferred by ambulance some two hundred yards to the Children's Theatre Block. A great deal more inconvenient for patients and staff was the return journey after surgery, with saline drips or blood transfusions attached to them, and a patient perhaps being sick, with all the disturbance of being moved about. It was a priority therefore to get at least one operating theatre in the Centre in a state where it could be used, and happily this was achieved some six weeks after the Centre had begun to function.

In the late autumn of 1997 a team from BBC TV in Scotland had requested permission to make a film of the day-to-day working of the Centre, which was to be shown on Scottish television at a prime time – 8 o'clock on the evening of Hogmanay, the last day of the year. This would be the best time, they explained, on such an auspicious occasion as Hogmanay, that the film could be shown, as folks would be relaxing after their turkey and plum-pudding dinner, and yet would not have reached the stage when the serious drinking of the evening would interfere with the effectiveness of what they were watching.

A number of additional Agency nurses had to be brought in temporarily to avoid the staff shortage that existed in the Centre being apparent, and the film that was made brought considerable acclaim to the Centre, and to the team who were running it – as well as bringing in contributions to help with the work of the Project itself.

The team that came out, with Dennis Cosgrove the producer, and TV newsreader Jackie Bird the commentator, made a splendid record of all aspects of the work of the Centre, including a brief tour of the wards with the surgeons examining, and talking with, the patients; and they also took discreet shots of non-gory operations being carried out.

At one stage in the team's visit, I was asked, as the instigator, to take part in a scene which involved me going about a quarter of a mile along a pebbly ocean beach, and then being filmed walking pensively back along the water's edge towards the camera. I tried to enliven the scene, and give it my best acting ability, by stopping to examine objects on the ground occasionally, and turning from time to time to gaze pensively at the sea. The whole affair, with the team bringing all its apparatus down onto the shore, took about an hour and a half but despite my own favourable impression of my acting ability, and the show I had put on, it was cut out entirely. So my hopes of a BAFTA award went down the drain!

Apart from the above, the TV team accompanied Mr Mork and me when we paid a visit to a Ghanaian village some ten miles out of Accra.

It was a typical Ghanaian village, no different from the hundreds of villages the length and breadth of the country, which clearly showed the poverty in which most of the patients who were seen at the hospital actually lived, with bare earth, and no paving or roads, and with mud-walled dwellings and thatched roofs. We had come to this particular village because it was known that Buruli ulcer, the comparatively recently discovered – and extremely disfiguring – disease, was rife amongst the children there.

As we drove along a lane running off from the main road we began to see small patches of vegetables and maize, obviously grown by the villagers, but pitifully small and stunted. Turning in at the entrance to the village, several small children – although there were a few obviously of school age – ran up towards the newcomers, but did not come closer than some fifteen to twenty yards, and stood there watching us disembark.

The local Health Officer, who had arranged to meet us and act as interpreter when we were looking at the patients, arrived just a few minutes behind us, and the children ran over to her shouting greetings, and crowded round the lady doctor's car. She was obviously very popular, and lifting up one of the smallest children, came over to greet us with the child in her arms.

We left the cars, and walked through the village to the house of the village Headman – a small wooden structure with a corrugated iron roof. As we approached he came out onto his small verandah – hardly more than a large wooden step in front of his doorway, with a palm-leaf layer held up with wire netting acting as a shade from the sun. The doctor introduced the film crew, Fabian and me, to him, and when I gave him the Ghanaian handshake he looked keenly at me, and then began to laugh, `You Ghanaian!' he exclaimed, and beckoned me to sit on a stool beside him, while everyone else sat on stools on the dusty ground – and some partly in the sun, but fortunately there was a canopy of high palm trees to shade them from the worst of it.

The TV crew were filming everything, and when they took a shot of the Headman he drew himself up – almost sitting at attention.

Once the niceties of the introductions had been completed, the doctor brought forward the patients for me to examine. Most of them were children around five or six, with one or two older ones, and I was astonished that none of them, with the evil-looking ulcers, mainly on their legs, though one or two of them had them on other parts of their bodies – and even on their faces – raw and red, with sometimes a rag also around a limb, seemed even moderately ill.

I was quite shocked to see so many cases in this one village, the only one with such a number of cases, and the doctor told me they came to her clinic five miles away for treatment with ointments as she found it impossible to persuade them to go into hospital, partly because of the cost, and partly because almost every patient who had been treated had had a recurrence of the ulceration – which was regretfully the classic history of this dreadful disease, for which no therapeutic cure had been found up till then.

It was a little disconcerting conducting these clinical examinations with the whole village standing around watching, but the activities of the film crew itself at least drew quite a lot of attention – particularly with the horde of non-affected youngsters who seemed to appear from nowhere.

One woman who was brought forward for me to see was carrying, almost concealed by a large shawl, a small baby, a little girl some eighteen months old, although she barely looked more than a year old at most. When it turned out it was the baby who was the patient, I was flabbergasted. I had no idea a child as young as this could be affected, and although the disease – which had involved almost the whole of one side of her face – was in the temporary healed phase, without any present ulceration, the disfigured side of her face and mouth were drawn right over to one side, making her breathing difficult, and I could not see how she could possibly be adequately fed. As I looked at this tiny deformed face, and tried to visualise the dreadful future that lay ahead for her, when congenital deformity still carries the stigma of wrong-doing in some quarters – even in Western communities – I almost wept.

Once I had seen all the patients, and we started getting into our various vehicles, two little boys came running up and started dancing about and shouting what we took to be `Goodbye'; it made an excellent final shot for the TV people, but I could still see the face of that disfigured little girl in my mind's eye.

The following day Jackie Bird was interviewing me – principally about the visit to the village – whilst sitting in the garden of the Novotel. When I came to the part about the deformed baby, and my astonishment at learning that this dreadful Buruli disease could affect such a young child – with the dreadful outlook I foresaw for this tiny baby – I found it difficult for a moment to go on speaking, and asked the camera crew to stop filming.

When the programme was eventually broadcast under the title `The Hospital That Jack Built', without any consultation with me, I discovered to my embarrassment that they had not stopped filming throughout the whole episode in the Novotel garden, and it appeared for the whole country to see.

I never heard anything further about the child, although we had offered, at the Project's expense, to bring her into hospital for an attempt at surgical correction of her deformity, and at least to improve her breathing and feeding problems. When one considered her bleak future, even after everything that could be done to help was done, and with the inevitability of the disease recurring in what was left of her face, one could only hope – despite the Hippocratic Oath – that without surgery to prolong her life and prevent the almost inevitable worsening of her breathing and feeding problems, she would not suffer for long.

In the planning of the Centre, the Burns Wing formed an important sector, with male, female and children's wards, as well as up-to-date treatment rooms, in one of which there was a saline bath and a patient hoist. Albert Paintsil, who was training in the UK, with special emphasis on the treatment of severe burns, was not due to return until August 1998, so severe burns and Buruli ulcers continued to be treated, at least initially, in the main Accident and Emergency Department, and came to the burns wards in the Centre quite late on when skin grafting was going to be required. Once Paintsil had finished the intensive training he was undergoing, the Burns Wing would be able to function as had been originally intended, and all the major burns which had hitherto been admitted to the Casualty Wards, where facilities were by no means ideal, would be treated from the start in the new Burns Wing – with a reduction in the complications, and even fatalities, that could occur when otherwise competent staff had to deal with the problems of severe burns.

When the Centre was opened, however, the available wards quickly began to fill up – and with the treatment of burns so nurse-intensive, requiring more than normal nursing availability, added to the existing serious nursing shortage, it was again probably just as well that the whole treatment of burns could not be carried out in the Burns Unit before Paintsil came back.

Apart from the problem with the Burns Wing, and although there were other problems in the running of the rest of the Centre without anything like the full complement of nurses, the number of patients admitted and treated gradually built up, and when, in early March, 1998, Her Royal Highness Princess Anne paid a visit to the Centre during a short stay in Ghana, the whole nursing staff, including those off duty, turned up to ensure that there was no noticeable lack of nurses in the wards. A limited party, including Martyn and Arthur, along with their wives, and senior hospital staff – and, of course, my own wife – were invited to meet the Princess personally.

When she had finally arrived at the entrance to the Centre (we had been in place for almost an hour), accompanied by the Minister of Health, Dr Brookman-Amissah, she laughed when I was introduced to her by the Minister and said, `So you're the man who causes all the trouble!' to which I replied, `But at least I get things done, Ma'am,' at which she simply laughed more loudly and moved on to the next person.

As she walked round the various wards I would introduce the doctor or nurse-in-charge to her, and then leave them to show her round while I went back out into the corridor where the senior hospital staff, the British High Commissioner and the Princess's security staff waited rather impatiently.

About half-way round her tour, the British High Commissioner asked me to try and speed things up, as she had another appointment after this – I understand on good authority it was the opening of a new Sewage Works – and she was running late.

When I went back into the ward I told the Princess I was getting pushed about timing. She laughed and said, `Tell them I make my own timing!' Which I did.

The High Commissioner nearly had a fit and squawked out, `Good Lord, Jack! You didn't tell her, surely?'

`Well, you told me to,' I replied, and walked back into the ward.

The background to her remarks about me making all the trouble had, I think, stemmed from a rather serious political situation which had begun when Dr Brookman-Amissah had, a few days before the Princess arrived, put a case to me for the new Centre to be considered, along with the Cardiac Centre and the newly opened Radiology Centre, as Centres of Excellence, and to become autonomous establishments, receiving grants and collecting fees.

A great deal of discussion had taken place about this, and the Minister appeared very much in favour of the possible arrangement. She finally asked me to prepare a Report on how I thought the Centre could function as an autonomous entity. My son David, who had saved the day regarding the opening of the Centre, had come out with his wife and mine, as honoured guests, for the Princess's visit, and I got him, Mrs Tay and Professor Yeboah to collaborate with me in drawing up the Report I had been asked for.

Professor Yeboah was due to retire from Head of the Surgery Department in the near future, and I had, with his approval, suggested that he might act as Co-ordinator or Director or whatever, to oversee the functioning of the Centre. The Minister, for reasons she did not disclose, was not prepared to accept this suggestion – we believed she had a newly appointed female hospital administrator in mind – and the upshot of the matter was that the whole concept of autonomy for the Centre and the designation of the three prospective Centres of Excellence was suddenly dropped, without a word of explanation. Hence I was `The man who causes all the trouble...'

Just what lay behind this matter of autonomy and Centres of Excellence is difficult to understand, for Dr Brookman-Amissah and I were on good terms, and once before, and again once after this visit of the Princess, she had attempted to help the Centre regarding its acute shortage of nurses by earmarking for the Centre, and sending me a copy of her list, of twenty nurses in training school who were about to graduate and were interested in working in the new Centre. When the actual graduation had taken place, many of the nurses who had been on the Minister's list came to see the Matron at the Centre, and were duly impressed with this brand new place to work in; but only one on the first occasion, and two on the second, actually joined the staff.

By October 1998, the number of nurses on the staff of the Centre had grown to twenty-five, and whilst it eased the workload on the staff a little to begin with, the number of patients in the wards gradually mounting offset any advantage the small increase might have brought.

Besides Mr Mork, Mr Tony Laing who, as explained earlier, had been working independently as a Consultant Plastic Surgeon in Korle Bu Hospital, had been accepted on to the staff when the Centre was opened, and inevitably this led to the further gradual build up of patient numbers, but because of the shortage of nurses the two blocks of wards, which had taken some six months after the Centre opened for the builders to complete, could not yet be brought into commission, and tended to act simply as storage space.

One encouraging event had been taking place during this difficult period, however, following President Rawlings' unscheduled injunction at the Opening Ceremony to the visiting group from Scotland to try and do something to counter the International Monetary Fund ruling that all medical treatment must be paid for, even by the poorest patients – who many times simply never came back for the operation or treatment prescribed after they had been seen at the Out-Patient Clinic and had learned what their treatment was going to cost.

Anne Mustardé, David's wife and one of the Project's Trustees, personally took up the challenge, and I shall shortly quote her own modest description of the task which, entirely on her own initiative, she undertook in response to the President's plea. The Patients Assistance Fund was set up in the summer of 1997, and achieved its objective of £100,000 by 1999!

As will be seen from Anne's statement, the original idea was to have the nurses try to assess who should qualify for financial help, but this had simply resulted in more or less every prospective patient claiming to be too poor to pay all, or even a part, of the cost of their treatment. For this reason the way in which the fund had inevitably to be administered was altered in the manner Anne describes. The only problem about this, and we could see no other way out of it at the time, was that when the prospective patients learned that the fund would not meet all the costs of their treatment, there were still substantial numbers, presumably of genuinely poor people, who never turned up for admission.

When one considers that the cost of one of the very fine catgut sutures (since replaced with equally expensive synthetic materials) with similarly fine needles swaged on, which are used in the deeper part of a wound in surgery of the face, and of which five or six might be used, is £7 *each*, and that the dressings, antibiotics and substances used in burns treatment are amongst the most expensive substances of that nature that are used – and for most patients with burns, there is the long-term stay in hospital, all of which the patient has to pay for – any help that Anne's fund could give, and will go on giving indefinitely, has been greatly appreciated.

Anne Mustardé's Report on the Patients' Assistance Fund

The Patients' Assistance Fund was set up with the aim of raising £100,000. It was to be invested in Scotland, and the income from this investment would be used to help poorer patients in Ghana pay for the materials during their surgery.

The sum was raised over a period of two years from a variety of sources; a television programme about the project shown on BBC Scotland generated many individual donations, both large and small, and applications to Charitable Trusts, and also illustrated lectures given by JM [JM being her father-in-law] to local groups, all helped to raise the profile of the work being done in Ghana and helped us to reach our target. Several donors supported the fund on a regular basis, some giving substantial amounts.

Initially the plan was to identify individuals who could not afford to pay for their surgery, but it soon became obvious that the administration of such a plan was not viable. Instead it was decided to purchase items used most commonly by the Centre, particularly materials used in the treatment of burns, without singling out individual patients for help, but making sure that those who could obviously afford to pay, did so.

A committee set up in Ghana oversees the ordering and distribution of the materials purchased by the fund.

CHAPTER 6

The ever-present problem of shortage of nurses, and the steps we had taken to cover up the true situation during the visit of the Princess, made me decide to take the matter up with the Director of the Department of Human Resources to see if he could hire additional nursing staff for employment in the Centre. (When the BBC Television crew had been making their film some nine months earlier, the Project had been forced to hire a number of Agency nurses for that whole week so as not to reveal to the film crew – and hence to the world at large – the lamentable situation regarding shortage of nurses.)

What worried me most was that there was always the possibility, whether it was correct or not, that part of the Centre might have to shut down; or even worse would be to find that the Hospital Administration staff, if they actually had the legal authority to do so, which I doubted would be the case, had transferred some of the surgeons from the main hospital, with its acute bed shortage, along with sufficient nurses to deal specifically with the patients they would bring to the Centre.

When I spoke to the Director of Human Resources (a doctor himself) he was very sympathetic, and actually quite enthusiastic, about advertising specifically for nurses to work in the Centre, but be paid out of the Ministry budget.

Following his advertisement he had several nurses making enquiries; but while they compared the Agency salary they were earning with what the Ministry paid, they never turned up, even for an interview, at the Centre.

After all the years of effort to develop Reconstructive Plastic Surgery for Ghana, and producing a magnificent building to house it, I could see a real possibility that our Ghana dream could ultimately collapse; and with the problems concerning the Centres much in my mind, it was most heartening to learn that in Kumasi the work of the Reconstructive Plastic Surgery Unit, following the difficult start-up in 1994 when Dr Pius Agbenorku had been accepted as Consultant Plastic Surgeon in Komfo Anoyke Teaching Hospital, had begun to pick up. It seemed that Pius was gradually developing his small RPSU, greatly helped, as described earlier, by the visits, albeit for only a few days, of the volunteer plastic surgeons who came from nine different countries, but at the beginning, mainly from the Plastic Surgery Unit in Canniesburn Hospital in Glasgow. These volunteers made the journey up to Kumasi a standard feature of their stay in Ghana, and although the objective of these trips to Kumasi was, of course, to help out with complicated surgical problems, it made a welcome break from the hustle and bustle of working in the overcrowded hospital in Accra.

With the passage of time Pius was gaining experience, particularly in the treatment of burns, but also in the handling of patients with Buruli ulcer, to which, for some unknown reason, the population north of Kumasi was particularly prone. (He was later to write an article on the subject, which was just beginning to be recognised for the world-wide tropical scourge that it had so recently become.)

As recounted earlier, of all the visiting surgeons who, from 1993 on, went up to Kumasi, Arthur Morris, Head of the Plastic Surgery Unit in Dundee Ninewells Hospital and lately President of the Scottish Branch of the British Medical Association, showed a particular interest in Pius, helping him to develop his small unit, and establish himself in a hospital which, until his advent, had had no trained plastic surgeon on its staff. In 1996, as one of the Trustees of the Project, Arthur put it to his fellow Trustees that in the future he would like to concentrate entirely on helping Pius to build up the Unit in Korafo Anoyte Hospital in Kumasi, leaving the stream of eager volunteers to continue to develop the Unit in Korle Bu Hospital.

His fellow Trustees unanimously supported Arthur's proposal, and, in fulfilment of the promise given to the Ashanti King on that first visit to Kumasi by the Argentine-Scottish team in 1992, a letter was sent to Professor Hiadzi, now retired from Head of Surgery but a close friend of the King, asking him to introduce Arthur and his wife Vicki to the Asantahene, and let Arthur explain personally to the King how we were carrying out what we had promised to do if we ever came back to Ghana.

It is a great pleasure to be able to record that the very considerable amount of time and effort Arthur had put in to the building up of a Reconstructive Plastic Surgery and Burns Unit in the Komfo Anoyke Teaching Hospital, was ultimately recognised by the University authorities in Kumasi by the conferring of an Honorary Professorship on him.

The details of the development of the Reconstructive Plastic Surgery Unit, including from the time Mr Morris took Pius Agbenorku under his wing, are best described by Arthur himself:

> As a volunteer in Ghana for the Reconstructive Plastic Surgery Unit (RPSU) Project, I went to Komfo Anoyke Hospital to visit the enthusiastic plastic surgeon Pius Agbenorku on 17 June 1994. He showed me round and took me to the then Head of the Department of Surgery, Professor Ni Amon Coti. Ni's attitude, berating me as a

'day tripper', sightseeing and not helping to get them a Unit 'like the one in Accra', stung me into a response. I felt a certainly sympathy, coming from Dundee, a peripheral city in Scotland. I knew that there was a tendency for the Capital to gain a disproportionate share of the resources.

I promised that when I came back to stay and operate, if they would provide facilities, I would do what I could to help: I did not know definitely then if I would return, but in January 1995, at my next visit, Ni was extremely impressed, and offered me lunch, and asked me to give a lecture to the Surgical Staff. A whole day operating list was laid on in the Polyclinic Theatre.

New impetus came with the appointment in 1995 of a new Head of Surgery, Professor Lawrence Addae Mensah. We decided to concentrate on burns treatment as a first priority as there was a massive need in a population base of five million plus. An area was designated on a long verandah for conversion to a burns intensive care unit.

In March 1996 Jack asked me to take Kumasi 'under my wing' and we decided to repeat the model of the Ghana RPSU Project with training of nursing staff a priority.

As a Rotarian I was able to secure additional funding to help the Kumasi Project from District 1010 – East of Scotland Rotary. We also applied for a Matching Grant from Rotary International to help train staff and provide equipment. The grant was awarded in 1998 for 15,000 US dollars.

Starting in 1996 six nurses were trained in Dundee in Specialist Plastic Surgery (three theatre and three ward nurses). After some delay the burns unit conversion was completed in autumn 2000 ready for the Opening Ceremony of the Burns Intensive Care Unit on 1 February 2001. It was up and running immediately.

In addition, full theatre equipment was provided for a plastic surgery facility for treatment of all types of conditions. In future an integrated Plastic Surgery and Burns Unit with en suite theatre is the prime goal and pressure is being brought to bear with the Hospital management team to bring this about.

To return to the situation in Accra: after Princess Anne's visit, and during the few days before we all went home, Maisie and I did some sightseeing with David and Anne, since David had seen very little of Ghana on his previous visit for the opening of the Centre.

The plan was to take a day off, and drive along the west coast to let David and Anne see what a stunning coastline it was, with the enormous breakers rolling up all the way from the Antarctic to crash down on the rocks and the sandy bays, and also to visit two of the castles that, like the one in Accra, had been built some three or four hundred years ago by various European peoples, to act partly as protected strongholds for the defence of the traders in ivory and gold, and partly as a secure place to hold these precious goods until they could be shipped back to their own country.

At a later date the main trading was in slaves, who were brought down from the hinterland and shipped, in many instances – at least at the beginning – to the developing colonies in North America. (It is worth mentioning again the fact that, contrary to what many Westerners believe, the slaves had not been forcibly taken from their villages by the foreigners themselves, but had been sold to the traders, either by conquering enemy tribes or by Arab middlemen who had bought them from these same warring tribes.)

Driving out westwards from Accra, past several small townships and eventually Winneba, the area where most of the non-Ghanaian ex-pats had their shore-side weekend villas, we were then able to turn south and head towards the shore road which was fringed all along the seaward side by groves of tall coconut palm trees. As we approached the shore-line it became obvious that the wind had dropped completely and there was hardly even a breeze ruffling the fronds of the palm trees.

But the astonishing feature that dominated the scene was the countless number of long, narrow fishing boats – some with outriggers, some with sails, although most had outboard engines fixed on a ledge on the starboard side of the boat – dotted about on the surface of the ocean as far as the eye could see. The second surprise was that, apart from these deep-water fishing boats, all along the shore, about every three or four hundred yards apart, were groups of individuals net fishing from the land with the aid of a net which must have been up to ninety or even a hundred yards in length, held firmly by a group stationed on the shore, and paid out from the stern of a boat which rowed round in a large circle before being brought back to a second waiting group a few yards from the first.

Once both ends of the net were on shore, each was dragged up the sand by a team of fishermen, their wives, and their older children, with the trapped fish leaping frenziedly about, and even sometimes leaping clean out of the net. With the whole catch ashore, the fish, about the size of small herrings, were laid out on reed mats on the sand in rows to dry out under the blazing hot sunlight. During the whole performance large numbers of hungry seagulls had converged on the scene, to be constantly chased off by the younger children. By evening, we were told, the dried fish would be gathered up and carted off to the fish merchant in one of the nearby villages.

The fisherfolk themselves lived in traditional dwellings grouped together under the shade of the palm trees, and made from bundles of reeds tied together for walls, while the roof was thatched, and all the way along the coast road we could see the little `villages' of these extended family groups under the palm trees – much as I imagine they have done for countless generations.

Although there were quite a number of villages along the coast itself, mainly involved in fishing, and a few small towns on the main Accra-Cape Coast road, Cape Coast itself was quite a sizable town, with its own Town Hall and a Hospital, and was the trade and business centre for the coastal area and a considerable part of the land between it and the range of hills to the north. We had a look at the hospital, for we had already had discussions about the possibility that in the future it might be feasible to start up a Reconstructive Plastic Surgery Unit here similar to the one in Kumasi.

The Castle was scarcely one's usual idea of a castle, and was a large rectangular building, with a central open square from which numerous apartments led off – quite a number of which had been occupied in recent times by Cape Coast civic authorities. A number of the apartments were open to the public, and typical African souvenirs could be purchased. From the defensive point of view there was, on the seaward side, a long open gallery with several ancient, rusty cannons still in place.

When the new trade in slaves had begun to develop, the owners of the castles had to construct dungeons, or other secure areas, in which the slaves could be held until a ship with suitably adapted holds called, and their destination was by then almost exclusively the developing colonies in both North and South America.

There were fortress/castles strung out all along the Guinea Coast of West Africa, but the two most famous were the one at Cape Coast and another at Elmina, some thirteen miles further west – and unless one had taken the coastal trip, and visited the two castles, one had missed seeing something quite unique to West Africa.

Of the two castles we had come to see, the one at Elmina, built on a huge rocky outcrop, was by far the more interesting – and the most macabre – since the huge dungeons where the slaves were kept, males in one, females in another, while awaiting transshipment, were better preserved, with iron rings still fixed into the walls above head height, to which recalcitrant slaves could be chained by the wrists. On the landward side of the castle, with the grim-looking gates through which the slaves passed to be forced on board the ships – many of them English – with their stinking, almost totally dark, holds, with no sanitation, and with only enough food to prevent them dying before they reached their destination, was the main fishing port for the whole of that part of the Ghanaian coast, and the waters of the harbour lapped up against the wall of the castle.

The harbour itself was well worth seeing, and there were literally hundreds of fishing boats tied up at any one time, all designed in the style of the original dug-out canoes, but extending anything up to seventy feet, and powered by one large Yamaha outboard motor mounted on a platform built out on the starboard side of the boat, a few feet before the stern itself. The sides of the boats were painted in brilliant colours with quite extraordinary individual designs, and the whole effect was as if one was looking at an enormous field of coloured flowers.

Having enjoyed the spectacle of the colourful harbour, we were walking back across the centre courtyard of the castle towards the entrance tower, when someone hailed me from the other side of the square.

`Hello Prof! I didn't expect to see you here!'

When I looked over to see who was speaking I recognised one of the administrative staff from Korle Bu Hospital. He walked across and I introduced him to the others.

`I heard that Princess Anne's visit to the Centre went off very well.' He went on, `You must have been pleased.' As the ladies began to move towards to the gateway he added, `I saw it a number of times while it was being built. It certainly looks splendid. You must be very pleased to know that all that was planned has come about.'

If he only knew...

Having had our fill of castles we woke up our driver, who was sound asleep in the back seat of the car, and had a word with him about our route back to Accra. On the journey from Accra in the morning we had caught glimpses of a range of hills to the north beyond a reasonably flat plain which, we thought, might be an interesting change of scenery to explore on the return journey.

There were several small streams running down from the distant hills and a lot of corn was being grown in irrigated fields, which gave a green appearance to the whole area – prompting David to say that, from what he had seen of the land, both today and on his trip to the Volta Dam, Ghana seemed to be very much greener than he had expected for a country right on the equator; and on reflection I realised that, with my own experience of other African countries, Ghana did seem a very green country, and had a definite attraction of its own, despite its small size.

The decision to detour inland, while giving us a chance to see something more of this fascinating country, was a mistake, however, for there was such a jumble of small roads, sometimes scarcely passable, which meandered so confusingly through small villages, that it was dark by the time we got back to the Novotel.

It had been interesting, however, and with the hills as a background, had given us a glimpse of Ghanaian country life we would otherwise have missed.

In the next few days the phrase, `all that was planned has come about' kept coming into my head, and gradually I came to see that it was indeed the situation and that my part in the Ghana Story had more or less been played out. Martyn had come more and more to the fore, and I had been encouraged that we were not building anything new any more, and Martyn was really the person who was running the Project; the Volunteers, the Ghana Patients' Assistance Fund, the continuing practical support given to Mork and Paintsil – and much more. Now, with Arthur Morris developing the Unit in Kumasi, it was obviously time for me to withdraw gracefully from the scene and let them get on with it. If only we could solve the nursing problem...

In a letter which I subsequently wrote to the Minister of Health I mentioned the fact that I was gradually handing over the running of the Project to Mr Webster and Mr Morris, and although I did not actually say so I implied that I was considering retiring towards the end of the year and leaving matters in the capable hands of these two.

The next visit to Ghana that I had arranged – and as usual had notified the Minister of my intention – was from the last week in June through into the middle of July, and two days after my arrival at the Novotel, I got a telephone message from the President's secretary saying that the President wished to see me at The Castle at 11 o'clock in two days time.

When I arrived at The Castle and made my way to Rawlings' private office, one of the uniformed officials came up to me and told me to follow him. Somewhat mystified at this change from the usual routine, I fell in behind him and we went across to another part of The Castle, where double doors led into the Presidential Audience Chamber, where I had previously been introduced to various dignitaries by Rawlings.

The official opened one of the doors and indicated that I should step inside, where I could hear a loud buzz of conversation taking place. As soon as I walked into the Chamber the noise immediately stopped, and I found myself looking at rows of silent Ministers and their deputies seated on the benches on either side of the Chamber.

Everyone was staring at me, and I felt extremely embarrassed standing uncertainly in the entrance until the official beckoned me forward and directed me to sit on the near side of the double-seated President's sofa-chair.

I had on previous occasions sat there by the President's side, but never with such an audience. Fortunately, within a couple of minutes Rawlings himself came into the Chamber, where everyone rose, including myself, and once he had sat down, he beckoned to me to sit alongside him.

At a signal from the President, Dr Brookman-Amissah, the Minister of Health, rose and began to rattle out `all the things I had done for Ghana'. It was extremely embarrassing, and I was not sure whether I would be expected to thank her or not. Fortunately, when Dr Amissah's speech came to an end, and before I had quite realised this was not simply one of her pauses, the President thanked her for what she had said, and called on two other dignitaries to say a few words.

When they had finished, Rawlings put his hand on my arm, reminiscent of that first time he had done so just over six years ago – and giving it a slight lift he nodded to me to reply now to the speakers.

I had realised that I would have to say something, and was trying to remember the points I wanted to make. In the event, I simply said it had been a most gratifying experience to have been the person who had had the opportunity of starting up what had grown, with the aid of so many helpers and supporters, into today's Centre of Excellence (and be damned with what Brookman-Amissah had decided – at least mentally). I thanked the President in particular for his constant guidance and support; and then just dried up – while the audience started clapping. The President then stood up, and obviously by prior arrangement, the Ministers and others began to leave the Chamber.

Once the last person had left, he said, `Right, Prof, leave your jacket and tie on the seat and come with me.' He had taken off his long outer gown, and in shirt sleeves and trousers led me, wondering what on earth this was all about, down a back stairway to the ground floor without saying a word. Opening the door he ushered me out into a small square of grass, surrounded by palm trees, on which stood an army helicopter with the rotor sweeping round purposefully, and creating quite a wind. As we ducked down and approached the plane the pilot got out of his seat and shook hands with Rawlings. Knowing as I did that Rawlings had at one time been a pilot in the Ghana Air Force, I was nevertheless reassured to see that the plane had its own pilot. Rawlings indicated to me to get into the seat next to the pilot's vacant one and to fasten my seat belt, and then, to my consternation, he lifted a flying helmet from the back of the helicopter and climbed into the vacant pilot's seat, put on his helmet, and strapped himself in...

As we rose from the grass I couldn't believe we could clear the palm trees on all four sides of us, but we did, and headed east along the coast at about four hundred feet. I had once owned my own plane, so I had a fair idea of the height at which we were flying. It was a beautifully clear day, and we flew as far as the Port of Tema, some twenty miles to the east of Accra, which was where our containers had been brought ashore, and then turned and flew directly back over The Castle, past Accra and on westwards for about another thirty miles, passing over the resort where expat. residents had their weekend villas, and then turned and flew back along the sandy shore, about a hundred feet above the water. Whenever we passed over children playing on the sands they would wave to the helicopter and dance about on the sand, and President Rawlings would wave back – and laugh as they did cartwheels and handstands in their excitement at the slow-flying helicopter travelling along so close to them and almost at eye level.

By now I had realised that this was Rawlings' way of saying thank-you to me, and had also realised that he was an expert pilot. I was thoroughly enjoying the flight – that is until we started to fly over Accra itself with the huge buzzard-sized scavenging vultures that floated past us as we flew at about three hundred feet across the city to have a look at the Centre, nestling beside the main Korle Bu Hospital. It was bad enough seeing these creatures floating by so closely, but every now and again the helicopter would give a sudden lurch to one side or the other as Rawlings swerved violently to avoid the occasional bird that flew in a panic the wrong way. To give him credit, we never hit any of them, but it certainly scared the daylights out of me.

When we finally came back over The Castle, I couldn't see our landing `field' at all at first, and then I began to make out what looked like a tiny green gap in the palm trees. The wind had got up since we had left, and the fronds on the palms were waving wildly in the breeze. I couldn't believe it was possible to get down through them on to the ground, and hoped we would have to divert to the nearby airport.

Rawlings, who I subsequently learned flew various types of aircraft as often as he could get the opportunity, was a real expert, and we landed with no problem.

As a thank-you/going-away present, I could not think of anything I could have been given to beat the flight we had just had – despite the birds. But I was not actually retiring – yet. I was just considering it as a possibility later in the year...

Regarding this question of retirement, it was interesting that for some time before the thought of actually retiring from the scene – which had in so many ways become a large part of my daily life, whether in Ghana or in Scotland – had arisen at all, I had, perhaps to some extent subconsciously, been putting more and more responsibility for managing the affairs of the Project in both countries on to Martyn Webster's shoulders. And as I took less and less responsibility for the running of the Project I began to feel that he should have some form of recognition for all that he was now doing, and the responsibility he was now carrying.

Ultimately, I decided to talk to Professor Yeboah about the matter: I thought that this was the best move, particularly in view of what he had said to me back in 1993 when the Project had first started to bring Reconstructive Plastic Surgery to Ghana at the request of the President. Yeboah had made it clear to me that a medical, or surgical, project of the nature and scope that we were hoping to develop, would only be recognised in Ghana if it was in the charge of, and was headed by, a Professor. As explained earlier, he had asked for information regarding any Honorary Professorships I held in Plastic Surgery – and on perusal of my credentials on that subject I was designated Professor in charge of the Project.

I thought that Martyn, a previous pupil of mine and distinguished in his own right (amongst other achievements being President of the prestigious European Association of Plastic Surgeons), might similarly be given the Honorary title of Professor since he was now effectively doing my job – and I put that to Professor Yeboah. He had no objection to my suggestion, but insisted that before Martyn could be given an Honorary Professorship by the University of Legone, in Accra, I would have to be appointed an Honorary Professor of the University first of all!

No amount of argument that, however much of an honour it might be to receive the Legone University Professorship, I did not seek this for myself – particularly since I was considering retirement – was accepted by Yeboah, and rather unwillingly I acceded to his instructions, with both Martyn and I applying for nomination for Honorary Professorships.

In due course we both received documents requesting nomination, to be filled in and returned to the Nomination Committee. One of the responses to be given was to supply the names and addresses of our principal teachers, so that they might be contacted for references. In all due seriousness I replied, `They are all dead.' And that was the last either Martyn or I ever heard about Honorary Professorships.

CHAPTER 7

In September 1998 Albert Paintsil – now Mr Paintsil since, like Fabian Mork before him, he had taken the opportunity while in the UK to sit, and pass, the FRCS examination in Edinburgh – returned to Ghana. With his special training in burns, as well as the training in Plastic Surgery in general, he would normally have been a very busy man but the shortage of nursing staff meant that the Burns Wing was not able to work at anything like its full capacity, and the addition of yet one more consultant imposed an added burden on the already overworked nurses.

In accordance with my decision to withdraw from the Chair and retire, my final visit to Ghana was in October, and on checking in at the Novotel I was told that Mr Watson, one of the volunteer plastic surgeons, was also staying there with his wife; but they had gone out for the evening, so I didn't meet them until the following day, Sunday, when they had the day off.

This was a first visit to Ghana for Tony and Anne Watson, friends of Martyn Webster, who had arranged this visit, and eventually I came across them at coffee time in the pool-side restaurant. Whilst they had much to say about their experience of working in the Centre, the conversation inevitably came round to the shortage of nurses, and the insoluble problem of attracting new nurses.

`But surely you realise why you are not getting new nurses?' queried Tony. I glanced at him to see if he was joking.

`If I had known the reason,' I told him, `we might have been able to do something about it.'

He looked at me with some surprise. `Every senior nurse,' he said, `when she finishes her training becomes a fully registered nurse, and expects to be offered on-site, low-cost accommodation – and the Centre doesn't have any: it's as simple as that...'

I could hardly take in what he was saying, for as far as I was aware, like myself, none of the volunteer surgeons had known anything about this.

`Why on earth didn't someone say so?' I asked.

He shrugged his shoulders, and with more than a hint of sarcasm said, `I can only assume that they all thought that the Big White Chief must have known what the problem stemmed from.'

At my suggestion we moved up to the privacy of my sitting room, where we discussed the problem at some length, and Tony eventually said, `It seems to me that the only way you could attract new nurses would be by renting accommodation and offering it to them at half the cost – or something like that.'

I could see this leading the Project into deep financial problems, and didn't agree with the idea at all; but he was so enthusiastic I said I would think about it. I had no intention of getting involved in anything like that, and eventually decided I would go to Korle Bu Hospital the following morning to talk to someone in the Nursing Administrative Staff about the problem.

At 8 o'clock on the Monday morning, without wasting time trying to make an appointment through the unpredictable hospital telephone system, I went along to the office of one of the Senior Nursing Officers. Having knocked and been told to come in, I asked the Nursing Officer about the information Tony Watson had given me. She simply confirmed that what he had said was correct, without expanding on the matter.

`Why didn't someone tell us about this?' I queried – perhaps a little too sharply. `Surely the Matron at the Centre must have known?'

Looking at me rather frostily, she said, `Of course she knew; and she also knew that the problem was the failure of your people to provide accommodation for the nurses; and she certainly knew that all the hospital's nurses hostels were completely filled with our own nurses.'

I had never heard of the hostels for the main hospital's nurses, but it seemed that, unknown to me, in the hospital's extensive grounds, some half a mile from the hospital itself and hidden by a rise in the ground, were twenty-eight nurses' hostels, each completely filled by qualified nursing staff – and families sometimes – from the main hospital.

This was staggering information, and my request – almost a plea – that some accommodation be made available somewhere for nurses who might then come to work in the Centre met with the sort of glare that only a Senior Nursing Officer can inflict on an importunate individual – especially a doctor. I left her office a great deal less aggressive than when I had entered, although I was most surprised at the distinction she had made between the nurses working in the main hospital and those working in the Centre – which I had always regarded as part and parcel of the rest of the hospital.

Everybody in the Centre – probably in the whole hospital – must have known about the nursing problem in the Centre, and nobody, for whatever reason, had had the sense to pass on the information I had just been given; and I had no idea who to turn to for advice, or how to tackle the problem.

Ultimately I had to give some thought to what Tony and Anne had suggested, but neither Mork nor the Matron in the Centre were very taken with the Watsons' idea, and they said that, first of all, rented accommodation was extremely expensive, and secondly, most landlords demanded half, or even all, of the year's rental up front. I told the Watsons what I had learned, the next time that I saw them, and speaking almost simultaneously, they said they would put £1,500 into the Project's bank account, if the Project would do the same, so as to meet the cost of the nurses' up-front payment; and the money could be recovered for future use by a weekly repayment from each nurse.

I was quite intrigued at their generosity (they were later to donate £4,000 to purchase a badly-needed replacement suction plant for the operating theatres).

Eddie Yeboah had been kept in the picture throughout this (and Martyn by fax), and I had told them about our discussions regarding the problem of attracting new nurses, but they were no help during my stay, for neither of them was enthusiastic about the idea of paying the total rent up front because of the difficulties involved in the collection of the `weekly rent' from the nurses. Yeboah said he thought that in the end we would have to build our own hostel – somehow...

The discussion about helping the nurses to meet the cost of renting, without the Project being saddled with any permanent monetary arrangement, went on by fax for the next few weeks, with no agreement being reached, and eventually, at the beginning of March 1999, I wrote to the new Minister of Health, my old friend Mr Samuel Nyamah-Donkor, explaining about the nursing shortage in the Centre, and telling him of the possibility of using the Watsons' money, doubled by our own greatly needed Project funds. There was actually no question of the Project being involved financially, but this I did in the hope that it would spur him on to say that the Ministry would offer to pay the up-front money; but I got no reply.

It is worth noting that in the months before I had sent the letter, several individuals had been continuing to look for suitable rental accommodation in order to make the Watsons' scheme work, but the prices being asked were astronomical, and with the rapid depreciation of the Ghanaian currency the whole plan was finally accepted as being out of the question as far as the Project was concerned.

In the end it seemed that Yeboah and Martyn had been right; and on 30 July I wrote again to the Minister, saying this time that if the Government would undertake to build a suitable twenty-four apartment nurses' hostel, I would defer retirement to try and raise the necessary funds. From a conversation I had with a builder friend the cost of a hostel for twenty-four nurses seemed likely to be the maximum I would have any chance of raising.

(Before all this had happened I was in fact in the process of formally relinquishing the Project Chairmanship to Martyn, partly because I felt I had accomplished at least the basis of what I had set out to do, but also because I owed it to my ever-loyal and long-suffering – but too often, lonely – wife. She later calculated that in the nine years I had by then been going out to Ghana (41 times), I had spent two whole years of our sixty-one years of married life in *That Ghana*...)

As the weeks went by, and I still had had no acknowledgement of my previous communications to the Minister, I sent, on 8 September, what I felt had to be the last request, asking whether he had received my letter regarding the Government building the hostel if I guaranteed the money to pay for it. Two days after I had sent the fax to the Ministry I received a letter(!) posted in Ghana on 2 September, from the Minister himself, and stating, amongst other things:

`My Ministry has no objection to the proposed plans to raise funds for this project, and is ready to lend the needed support when the need arises.' And further down, `I am by this letter informing you of the Ministry's acceptance of your proposals under reference, and looking forward to hearing from you.'

That same day I sent a fax to the Minister thanking him for his approval of my offer to raise the funds, while the Ministry would be responsible for the construction of the building. I asked that he would appoint one of his deputies to take charge of this, and he faxed me back saying he had put the whole matter, apart from the fund-raising, in the hands of Mrs Victoria Dako, the Director of Health Administration and Support Services in the Ministry of Health. Being acquainted with the lady personally I knew that I need have no further worries on that score.

Apart from his remarks regarding building a nurses' hostel, in his letter of 2 September, the Minister had also said, `We are also arranging to post some of the newly trained nurses and others recruited from the regions to open the Burns Unit.' I had no idea where the additional nurses were to be accommodated, but the main thing was that, with Albert Paintsil having returned from the UK, it meant that at last he would have enough staff to bring all burn cases, including the extensive ones which he had had to deal with in the main hospital, into the Centre under his constant care.

At the time when I received the Minister's last fax I was very involved with the preliminary problems of getting the hostel constructed, and I never did find out where the new nurses were accommodated. The main thing was that they were there working in the Centre.

To return to the matter of building our own hostel, I had told the Minister that, while I would accept whichever architect/contractor he decided on, I sincerely hoped that it would not be the one who built the Centre, and I was greatly relieved when I received a fax informing me that I was free to choose the architect myself.

Whilst I was delighted at the contents of his letter of 2 September, and the injunction to proceed, my main worry now was to obtain some idea of how much a hostel that would hold twenty-four nurses would actually cost. I was very much aware that I would need to be reasonably sure that I would be able to raise the money before anything further was arranged. (I was a little older than when I had been able to make the preliminary telephone arrangements, and then see seven or even eight prospective contributors in a day; and in any case, I didn't like the idea of going back a second time to anyone I had already visited, begging cap-in-hand; and to obtain the sum we were likely to have to find, this would simply have to be done.)

Finally I decided to contact my old friend Alex Kujiku, who, as a quantity surveyor, could presumably price whatever tentative design I had in mind. In the discussions I had with Alex, by fax and by phone, we considered the costs for having twelve two-bed rooms with communal toilet area, kitchen and lounge facilities, and also another plan with twelve separate flatlets, each containing two bedrooms, and each sharing toilet facilities, kitchen and sifting room; but when these suggestions were put to the nursing staff in the Centre for approval, there were apparently loud protests that we had made no provision for individual self-contained flatlets for older, more senior staff!

In the end we decided on a plan showing six self-contained flatlets for the older nurses, and nine two-bedroom units sharing toilet and other facilities. When this was costed by Alex, however, it was going to be well over £110,000, which effectively ruled it out until Alex suggested we have a three-floor building with two flatlets and three two-bedroom units on each floor which, with the much less extensive ground plan, would cost around £90,000-£100,000, a sum which, in view of the urgent need to take on more nurses, I decided I would be prepared to take on.

By this time it was January in the Millennial Year, and although, at 83, travelling was getting more of a problem, I felt it was necessary for me to go out to Ghana, principally to deal with the matter of choosing a suitable architect, but also to make sure we would get a suitable site, close to the rest of the nurses' hostels.

I was given various people's views on the merits or otherwise of a number of architects, and I happened to mention the difficulty of making the right choice to Mr Vostok, the MD of Dizengoff Ltd., who had put in the air-conditioning units in the two operating theatres in the Centre. He told me that the best man he knew for this comparatively less extensive type of job was a Mr Amponsah, and he arranged for me to have a talk with him about the proposed hostel.

When I eventually met Mr Amponsah I was very taken with him, and on receiving further confirmatory good reports concerning his professional thoroughness, I spoke to the Minister about the situation. As a result, Mr Nyamah-Donker instructed Mrs Dako to have one of the architects on her staff, Mr Vanderpuye, meet with me and Mr Amponsah in her office.

After a very full discussion of what was proposed, Mr Amponsah retired from the room, and it was agreed by Mrs Dako and myself that the contract should be assigned to Amponsah Ltd, with Mr Vanderpuye acting as my representative and reporting to both Mrs Dako and myself once a week on progress with the building.

Amponsah and I got on well, but when the two of us met to discuss in more detail the building he would construct, and which he had costed at $165,000 (£110,000) at the current rate of exchange) I said initially that that was out of the question. (It had been agreed with Mrs Dako that all payments would be made in US dollars on account of the constantly depreciating value of the local currency.) I was advised independently however that it was most unlikely that I would be able to find anyone else who would be any cheaper, so the contract was duly offered to Amponsah.

For all his straightforwardness – and fairness, as I was to discover – Amponsah was nevertheless a very astute individual, and on hearing that twenty-four nurses was about half of our ultimate goal, he suggested that if he built the three-storey hostel in the form of a right angle, with one short arm and one long arm, it might be that at a future date the Centre might be in a position to build a mirror image const-ruction facing the original one, producing a secluded inner square where the nurses could relax in total privacy!

He had also said that by altering the ground dimensions slightly – which he could do using the L-shape – he could build three identical flats, each housing nine nurses, and thus bringing the total to twenty-seven, still for $165,000 – which, when he had explained this, justified me, in my own mind at least, in taking the plunge! By my basic arithmetic, with twenty-four rooms at £6,500 each, this arrangement would give us three greatly needed rooms for nothing.

While I doubted the Project would ever be in a position to build a mirror image hostel, I held my counsel, and having seen tentative plans and drawings which he had made, I agreed to his three-floor L-shaped design, and the contract was eventually duly signed by Mrs Dako on my behalf on 1 April 2000.

Although finding a suitable architect/contractor (and a good site) was the main reason for my visit, of almost equal importance was the raising of funds, and in relation to that there had been a most extraordinary beginning in Scotland. This had involved a friend of mine, Ian McNee, who had lived near me in Glasgow in the days before I ended up in Ayr, and who had previously given several donations to the work of the Project in Ghana.

On hearing about our plans for building a nurses' hostel for the Centre – and the reasons for doing so – he contacted me, telling me that his wife had died recently and that he wished to make a contribution to the hostel fund. To my astonishment I received a cheque for £20,000! As a registered Charity the project was able to collect a further £9,000 return of Income Tax, and I reckoned this wonderful gesture had paid not far short of a third of our total cost. With this information I contacted, whilst I was in Ghana, the MDs of several of the leading banks in Accra, who had all helped modestly in times past, and having told them about the Scottish donation of £29,000 asked them to make a generous contribution to enable us to build this all-important nurses' hostel.

Every one of them seemed to be prepared to donate a substantial sum, and I subsequently received a letter from the Secretary of the Association of Bankers, saying that at a meeting of the General Council one of the bankers with whom I had mainly been in touch tabled the financing plan to help with the building of the proposed nurses' hostel by the Project. He was pleased, he said, to inform me that the General Council of their Association was `favourably disposed to donating handsomely to the project'. They had, however, deferred the decision on the quantum of the donation to their next meeting, scheduled `some weeks ahead'.

I began to speculate on what a `handsome' contribution would amount to – knowing as they did about my Scottish friend's substantial donation. I was relieved that, with any luck, I would not have much more of the rather undignified fund-raising to do. When the AGM of the Bankers Association finally took place, however, it seemed that, as far as I could interpret the matter from a letter I received from the Secretary of the Bankers' Association, the rank and file membership took exception to a small number of their members making a unilateral decision on their own and vetoed any donation at all! Three of the `Big Banks' did ultimately make a contribution, but jointly it amounted to a total of $5,000.

This was a shattering blow to my calculations of the likely balance I would still have had to find if the Bankers' Association had contributed `handsomely', and it added greatly to the problems now encountered of having to ask for contributions – often, whatever decisions I had earlier made, or reservations I might still have about it, from people I had already been to see – but it would have to be done.

The Korle Bu Hospital Administration had actually allocated a suitable site near to the rest of the nurses' hostels, and had cleared the decision with the Ministry of Health, who were the owners of all the land on which the hospital complex was built, and on 20 April the Foundation Stone was laid by Dr Adibo, now an adviser to the Minister himself, and the work of laying the new foundations commenced. One of the complications of this last was that the site was criss-crossed by deep foundation trenches and intervening mounds of spoil, obviously intended at one time to have been unusually deep foundation trenches for a fairly tall building which, for some reason unknown to Amponsah, had been abandoned. It was no great problem to fill these trenches using the existing spoil, but it would have been interesting – and useful – to have known at the beginning just why the site, which seemed to be in a prime spot, had been abandoned.

Levelling the site was just the start, however, of unexpected problems that Amponsah had to cope with as the building work proceeded, and the first major one was when a channel had been dug and a drain was being laid to connect the hostel to the local drainage system. When the existing drainage, with its very rusty manifold, was opened, it was discovered that the whole local drainage system had irretrievably collapsed and had obviously been abandoned, which accounted for the large pool of stinking water, some seventy yards from the hostel site, that appeared on the surface occasionally – and provided a perfect breeding ground for mosquitoes.

Amponsah reckoned that the least expensive, and indeed the only practicable, way round the problem, was to construct a huge septic tank to the side of the building site. He put in a second tank, close to the first, on the grounds that it would save money when we came to build the mirror-image hostel!

Apart from the drainage problem, the building work was eventually proceeding according to plan, and with no major snags arising. Mr Vanderpuye faithfully sent me copies of his weekly reports and the progress being made, and on 20 June 2001 I was delighted to learn from him that the work was actually ahead of schedule with 15 per cent carried out already.

In the meantime, in the Centre itself, with the Burns Wing now being almost fully utilised with the aid of the additional nurses the Minister had arranged to work there, there was a happier outlook for the whole staff, surgeons as well as nurses, with the knowledge that the hostel should be functioning by the beginning of the year 2001. With a continuing corresponding increase in the number of patients admitted, the existing open wards were now almost at capacity level. (The wards forming the two late-finished parts of the building were still not being used for their intended purpose, and the surgical staff of the main hospital seemed to have forgotten about the male and female leg ulcer wards – at least for the present – but opening more wards without a corresponding increase in nurses was not at that time an option.)

There had been an encouraging number of donations received, mostly from sources in Scotland, including a further substantial contribution from a Trust in Edinburgh which over the eight years donated £40,000, and it seemed that, if donations continued to reach us at this level, we should have no difficulty in meeting the full cost of the hostel. The donations were received not only from wealthy sources, but also from people who donated modest sums, and in some cases more than once.

There was one lady, Miss Bessie Allan, who owned a shop in a small town to the south of Glasgow, and she apparently kept a jar on her counter with a note saying that the contributions – mostly change being received – were going to help the Project provide a Reconstructive Plastic Surgery and Burns Centre in Ghana; and every now and again I would receive a cheque from her, with the sums ranging from around £5 to £20, which I acknowledged along with some remarks on how the money was being used. Over a two year period, this amounted in total to over £200!

In the Centre itself, the care of patients less able to pay for their treatment was greatly assisted by a decision made by the Parish Church in Alloway which my wife and I attended, to celebrate the Millennium year by donating £1,000 each month to help the poorer patients with the cost of surgery. Mr Paintsil acted as the contact in the Centre and he sent reports each month of the patients who had been operated on. By the end of the year there was still £1,000 in the fund the Church had set up, and this was also sent out to Ghana – making a total of £13,000. While this money did not go to augment the funds being gathered for the purpose of paying for the new hostel, it had greatly extended the work which the Ghana Patients Assistance Fund was set up to do.

In September of the Millennial year, President Rawlings paid a non-State visit to Britain, and to my surprise I received an official invitation to a luncheon being given in his honour in Lancaster House, adjoining Green Park.

Not wishing to risk some hitch if I flew up to London on the morning of the luncheon, I flew up the evening before and stayed at a flat in Chelsea owned by my son David and his wife.

Next morning, with plenty of time on my hands, I took the Underground to Green Park and sauntered along in the sunshine to Lancaster House.

I must have been one of the few guests, if not the only one, who arrived on foot, and it was quite amusing watching the Rolls Royces and Daimlers, with a sprinkling of taxis thrown in, queuing to drive up to the huge ornate doorway and discharge their passengers. For a few moments I stood looking at the politicians and well-heeled businessmen and their ladies dismounting and walking up the broad stairway. Within minutes a policeman came up and very politely said, `I'm sorry, Sir, but you cannot stand here.' And it suddenly dawned on me that, as the only person not coming out of a car or taxi, I must have appeared to him to be a member of the public who should be standing out on the street if they wanted to watch the guests arriving.

I brought out my official invitation, and as soon as he saw it he said, `I'm sorry, Sir, but you still cannot stand here, and I must ask you to go inside.'

Muttering my apology for the breach in etiquette I went in, and followed the line of guests up the main stairway, from the top of which the queue shuffled steadily towards where our hostess was standing welcoming the guests, and guiding them through an open glass doorway, beside which she was standing.

I must have looked a great deal older than I felt, for she put her hand on my arm, and saying, `Be careful of the step!' she guided me out onto a large balcony crowded with guests.

In the distance I could make out a queue of guests waiting their turn to be introduced to the President – many obviously Ghanaians – and with a welcome cool gin and tonic in my hand, I stood looking at the other guests nearby, none of whom I knew – but it was interesting to see how the other half of the world lived, and to learn what the various stocks and shares were doing.

After about half an hour, an announcement was made to the effect that we should make our way to the State Apartment in which lunch would be served.

The room itself was much larger than I had expected, with a long top table flanked at either end by an equally long side table, and gradually everyone, except those at the top table, found their place cards and were duly seated. While awaiting the guests at the top table there was a general buzz of conversation. I was seated at the very bottom of one of the long side tables, and my attempts at conversation with my only neighbour – on my left – got little more than a `Nice to meet you,' once he had ascertained that I was neither some foreign tycoon, nor an obscure Scottish nobleman he had never heard of and of course there was no one beyond me with whom to carry out more of this going nowhere conversation.

Suddenly one of the uniformed staff came into the room, looked abruptly round, and walked over to where I was sitting, more or less twiddling my fingers and wondering how so many of these people seemed to know each other so well.

'Excuse me, Sir,' he said. 'May I ask if you are Professor Mustardé?'

I said that I was; whereupon he went on, loud enough for the rest of the guests to hear, 'President Rawlings would like to speak with you, Sir. Would you be good enough to come with me?'

There had been a sudden hush when the messenger had first spoken to me, followed by an absolute babel of voices wondering who on earth this man that the President wanted to speak with, as I rose from my seat and crossed over the room in his wake.

My guide led me down a long corridor, at the end of which I could see our hostess – standing beside the President and his wife. As I came up to them she said, 'The President is very cross with you for not going to speak with him on the balcony.'

I was quite astonished at what she said, and I turned to Rawlings. 'Sir,' I said apologetically, 'I have the privilege of speaking with you every time I am in Ghana and to be frank, I thought it a little unfair if I took up a place in the queue of people waiting to be introduced to you.'

Rawlings smiled and said, 'Look Prof, any time you and I are at some function or other, you must come and speak to me.'

I glanced over towards our hostess, who laughed, and muttered, 'Well, that's you told off all right.'

Rawlings then turned to his wife and said to her, 'You know the Professor, of course,' and without opening her mouth, she held out her gloved hand, which I shook, while saying, 'Good morning, Ma'am.'

Turning to the official who had brought me – now standing at a discreet distance while our little *tête à tête* had taken place – our hostess asked him to take me back to where the luncheon guests were impatiently waiting for Rawlings and the other top-table guests to appear.

On my return to my seat at the luncheon table, all conversation stopped dead, and I could feel everyone's eyes on me, wondering who on earth was this unknown character who was evidently so close to the President? Fortunately our hostess, accompanied by President Rawlings and his wife, as well as the other top-table guests, came into the room at that moment and the buzz of conversation stopped immediately.

As I had walked back down the long corridor I remembered the time, so many years ago, when, while on one side of a large room I had been explaining to President Rawlings what the Project could do to give Ghana its own Reconstructive Plastic Surgery Unit, on the opposite side of the room the First Lady had, I later learned, been discussing cosmetic surgery with Alberto Ferriols, from Argentina. The First Lady and I had not spoken to each other on that occasion, nor had I ever met her again until today in London, when she did not utter a word.

I hoped, for everyone's sake, that the Argentina Matter was no longer a problem.

By the autumn of that year, however, donations to fund the building of the nurses' hostel, both in Ghana as well as in Scotland, had begun to dwindle considerably, and after payment to the builder of the various tranches which were due to him, the building fund had dropped by October to a point where at least £10,000 would need to be found to pay the builder in full by the end of the year, when the Opening Ceremony was supposed to take place – and there would still be the £9,000 retention fee six months later. Amongst those people who I had contacted in Ghana earlier on regarding funds for the building of the Hostel had been the new Japanese Ambassador, but he was in Japan at the time, and having heard nothing, I was loathe to contact the Embassy again since Japan had, over the years, donated expensive equipment to the project and, of course, had paid for the whole operating-theatre suite in the Centre.

On a day when, at home in Scotland, I was feeling particularly concerned about the deficit that was almost certain to occur, I received a fax from Ghana saying that the Japanese Ambassador was going to match the £29,000 my Scottish friend had donated at the very beginning of the Hostel episode! How true the quotation: 'The Mills of God grind slowly.'

At first all I could think about was the certainty that the builder could be paid in full, but in time, as the initial euphoria began to settle down, I began to realise that we were going to have some £10,000 on our hands after everything had been paid for, and I began to think a little further...

I contacted Amponsah and asked if it would be possible to add a small fourth floor that might give us rooms for another three nurses? I told him about our windfall, and asked if what I was requesting could be carried out within the figure of £10,000.

He said he would have to go over the figures concerning the depth and width of the foundations with regard to the added weight they would have to bear, and also calculate whether the walls would take the added pressure from a fourth floor. In the end he said that he would be able to add a fourth floor, less extensive than the other three, and with accommodation for six nurses, each two sharing kitchen and other facilities, and we could have this at a specially reduced cost of an additional $20,000 (£13,300)! This would give us accommodation for thirty-three nurses, and would only put up the total cost of the hostel to $186,400 (£123,000) – leaving just a comparatively small sum still to find.

Amponsah's generosity sprang, I am sure, from the fact that, amongst other reasons he may have had, he was very supportive of what the Project had given Ghana, and he was genuinely interested in doing all he could to help the work we were involved in – as were the members of his Church, he had once told me.

The year 2000 had been of significant importance as far as the bringing of this special branch of surgery to West Africa was concerned, by reason of a Teaching Course in this speciality which Mr Webster and Mr Morris organised in Accra, assisted by Professor Yeboah and Mrs Tay, and regarding which Mr Webster supplied the following information:

> The first Instructional Course in Reconstructive Plastic Surgery and Burns was held at the International Conference Centre in Accra in March 2000. Billed as the 'Pan African Course in Plastic Surgery' it attracted participants from Nigeria, Sierra Leone, the Ivory Coast and Kenya, but mostly from Ghana itself. A total of 86 participants attended lectures covering the whole scope of reconstructive techniques from simple grafting to micro-surgical free tissue transfer and craniofacial surgery.
>
> Professor Achebe from Nigeria represented the West African College of Surgeons, and the Reverend Professor Seth Ayettey, Provost of the College of Health Science of the Postgraduate Department of the University of Ghana, was also in attendance.
>
> Lecturers from the United Kingdom and the European Community, together with local experts in the subject, worked with the participants for five days, giving didactic lectures and holding seminars. The Course was voted a great success and played an important part in the training of new surgeons to undertake this work in Ghana and West Africa. More Courses are planned.

One jarring note, as far as construction of the Hostel was concerned, was the discovery by Amponsah, shortly after starting work on the foundations, that the antiquated electricity transformer serving the area was insufficiently powerful enough to take on the added load of supplying electric power to the Hostel! It turned out that there were four nearby nurses' hostels which had been completed almost four years ago but had lain empty all this time because the transformer was not able to supply them with electric power.

As the hampering effect of not being able to use any electrically-driven tools slowed down the work of building `Our Hostel', it became obvious that the original opening date would have to be postponed from the end of the year until some time in the year 2001.

Once the initial shock of this discovery had died down, Amponsah said that, if need be, he could lay an underground cable to a source outside the hospital grounds – but it would be costly – and accordingly the building work on the Hostel carried on in the hope that `Something would be done by the Hospital Board'.

CHAPTER 8

When the transformer problem had first been identified, shortly after construction of the Hostel for the nurses working in the Centre had begun, it had been officially accepted that a more powerful transformer would have to be installed, not only in order that the Hostel for the Centre could be completed and brought into use, but also to open up the four empty hostels so badly required by the main hospital.

But the months had gone by and the new transformer never appeared, despite repeated assurances that it was definitely going to be installed, and the problem, already referred to, of the delaying effect that this would have on the anticipated opening date of the Hostel before the end of the year, threw all the tentative plans for an Opening Ceremony into total disarray.

From my own point of view, at the age of 84, any marked delay could raise problems. For whilst the twelve-hour journey from Glasgow to Ghana was simply tedious, I was beginning to find the return journey through the night on a Saturday or Sunday (non money-begging days) was becoming more and more of a strain which took a day or two to pass off, with a completely filled economy-class section seemingly consisting entirely of families with crying children, who went on crying all night – at least it seemed like that. But it was our Opening Ceremony, and I was prepared to make the journey one last time to attend it – only, however, if the new transformer was installed and working, so that we could be sure the hostel had a full-powered electrical system actually functioning. (On a few occasions when a business class seat had been available because of a no-show, Mr Westerman, the Regional Director of KLM, had arranged to upgrade me to the vacant seat, but at the week-ends there was no guarantee of that, and in any case there might be others prepared to pay the full cost of an upgrade.)

During my last routine fund-raising visit to Ghana at the beginning of October, there had been much discussion about the question of furnishing the new hostel, and an estimate of the cost of providing beds, armchairs, tables, plus a cooker and a refrigerator – one set for each senior nurse's apartment, and one set, plus an extra bed, for two nurses sharing a toilet and other facilities amounted to between £10,000 and £12,000, and whilst I suggested to Mr Amponsah that perhaps his Church and mine might contribute towards this, nothing came of any discussion with him on the subject and it looked as if we were back to the position, which was getting more and more difficult to carry out, of trying to squeeze funds from whatever sources had not been targeted already.

Fortunately, someone who had heard about this latest problem made a point of contacting me and explaining that the nurses themselves looked on their job, and therefore their accommodation, as more or less theirs for a long time and preferred to bring their own furniture – and in the case of the senior ones, paying for an individual flatlet, it was apparently accepted that they would bring their own personal cooker and refrigerator.

This welcome information, which was checked out and found to be the normal custom, had a snag, however, in our own case, where the twin-bedrooms with sharing of facilities were concerned, for there would be the question of which individual would supply the cooker or stove, and more particularly, the fridge.

A small stove was apparently not a great problem for one or both `tenants' to provide but a refrigerator was a different matter, and in the end a decision was taken that the Project would supply a modest-sized refrigerator for each of the shared apartments.

As the building work continued, Mr Amponsah had warned me that, with the problems of lack of power to drive electric saws and drills, plus the fact that a fourth floor had been added to the time schedule, while work on the outer walls and the roof would be completed by the end of the year, the inside plastering and joiner work would take considerably longer – possibly a further six weeks, depending on when, and if, the new transformer was installed.

At the beginning of January 2001, I received the welcome confirmation that a new, more powerful transformer was now installed, and the four empty hostels, as well as our own, were receiving a normal electricity supply. Along with this long-awaited good news came an official Government communication informing me that the Opening Ceremony would take place on Tuesday 30 January!

It appeared, from the information I was given, that this was a totally different matter from the Opening Ceremony when the Centre had been involved, and where at no time had the Project been regarded as anything other than the main fund-raiser to augment the Ghanaian Government's own contribution.

I had thought that when I finally accepted the completed Hostel from the builder (Mrs Dako was going to act in this case on my behalf), I would officially become the Owner, or Client, since the money to pay the building had all passed through my hands, and I expected it would be a straightforward exchange of documents and signatures – which Mrs Dako could have dealt with on her own, and without me having to be there. But the situation now was apparently that, as the Hostel (with written agreement that it would be used solely for nurses working in the Centre) was going to be gifted to the Ministry of Health, acting on behalf of the Government of Ghana, I was now technically the Donor, and since the donation was being made to the Government of Ghana, there were formal documents to be signed jointly by myself as Donor and by Dr Mensah as Director-General, Ghana Health Service.

Within days I received several lengthy official documents, under an initial heading *Handing Over Memorandum of Understanding.*

This made the Opening Ceremony the Government's business, and it was to be conducted with a degree of formality I had not anticipated; but at least I could better understand why what had seemed a rather peremptory way of letting me know on what date it was all going to happen had been sent to me; and I suppose Tuesday 30 January had been the most suitable date for the Government personnel who would be receiving the gift of the Hostel.

For personal reasons, however, that particular date was by no means suitable from my point of view, for it was imperative that I should be in Glasgow on Wednesday morning, 31 January, but there was nothing I could do about that, and I purchased a ticket, flying out on 23 January to give me an opportunity to say `Thank you' and `Goodbye' to all those who had helped to make my hopes and expectations come true, and returning overnight on the 30th.

On the morning following my arrival in Accra on Friday 26 January 2001 for the opening of the Centre's Nurses' Hostel, and my last visit to Ghana, I had met Mr Amponsah at the building site, and was most impressed by the appearance of the Hostel. It was so totally different from the nearby collection of main hospital hostels, which were simply white-painted rectangular boxes, with completely flat roofs – good at least for putting washing on – all identical and crowded together like a military barracks.

`Our Hostel', which, with its decorative, guttering-edged red-tiled roof and walls of a natural stone colour – and with the unusual, but actually quite attractive L-shape removing any suggestion of a rectangular box – looked almost like a Mansion House or a hotel, with its distinctive architecture, and although it formed only half of a square, the area at the back of the building already gave the impression of shelter and privacy totally lacking in the open rows of the main hospital's characterless rectangular boxes.

I congratulated Amponsah on the pleasing appearance of the building, in front of which an adequate-sized car park was being constructed. I had noted at the entrance to the larger of the two parts of the building that there was a plaque which had an inscription JAPANESE BLOCK on it, while a similar plaque, reading MCNEE BLOCK, was placed on the entrance to the smaller part of the building – in recognition of the two contributors who had done more than anyone to make what I was now admiring, possible.

When we went into the buildings (although adjoining, there was no internal communication between what was virtually two separate constructions) there were obviously a few final touches to be added – door handles and the like – and certainly the place was going to require a thorough clearing out before the Big Day.

As we walked through the two ground floors – I had no intention of going up any stairs – I could see how much more expansive the individual senior nurse apartments were than I had expected, and likewise the communal areas of the two-bedroom, and occasionally three-bedroom, flats (depending on the shape of that part of the building), now that they had walls and a ceiling, which seemed to extend them.

Quite obviously the building was going to be in a complete state of readiness at the handing-over Ceremony on the following Tuesday, and as we walked round the outside of the building, which also had some tidying up to be done on it, my companion stopped and turned to face me. I could tell immediately that whatever he was going to say was bad news of some sort, and I suddenly realised he had been giving me the very impressive tour as a lead-up to having something to tell me which I was going to find less pleasant.

There was a low stack of skirting boards under a lean-to roof nearby, and waving a hand towards them, he said, `Let's sit down in the shade.' I couldn't for the life of me imagine what he was going to say when, as far as I could tell, everything looked ready to start up immediately after the Opening Ceremony.

`We connected up the water supply to the fourth floor last week,' he said, looking up at the top of the building, `And we have discovered that the water pressure is too low for anything but a trickle to reach there!' For a moment the implication of what he had just said didn't quite register with me, and as I turned my gaze towards the top floor he went on, `It means putting in water tanks in both parts of the building in order to collect the drip feed; and to give a reasonable flow on the top floor itself they will have to be situated in the attic – which will mean strengthening the floor, and possibly the walls and the ceiling of the floor below.'

As the full implication of what he had been telling me began to sink in, I had a cold feeling in my chest. I managed at length to ask, `Does that mean that all this business of the Opening Ceremony is cancelled? And what on earth is it going to cost?'

`No,' he replied. `The Ceremony will go ahead as planned – it's a Government thing, with the Hostel being gifted, and it could be months before it could be set up again with Government and other guests attending – and the Government, through the Ministry of Health, is going to carry out the work – and meet the full cost...' I closed my eyes and heaved a sigh of relief – I had just about had enough of incidents like this.

The upshot of the matter was that, through Mrs Dako, Amponsah formally handed over the building to me as the Client, just as if the building was now ready to be used, and he eventually received from me the first of two tranches of the five per cent retention money which had been held back at the time of each payment, in accordance with the contract.

On the Tuesday morning, 30 January, the Opening Ceremony went ahead, with about two hundred participants and guests, including the Japanese Ambassador, Mr Nitta, as if nothing untoward had happened. The press were there, taking shots of the Government and Ministry of Health officials, the Chairman of the Governing Body of Korle Bu Hospital and others.

Doctors from the hospital and senior nurses were also present, and in due course, after I and Dr Mensa, the Director General, Ghana Health Service, had signed the official papers, donating the Hostel to the Government of Ghana, it was duly declared open.

Following this we all trooped through the ground floor, first of the Japanese and then of the McNee blocks, had more photographs taken, and eventually moved up to the main hospital for refreshments.

If the delays in the opening of the Nurses' Hostel had been something of a let-down, there had been one item of really good news which raised our spirits enormously.

On 1 February 2001, a landmark occasion took place in the Komfo Anoyke Hospital in Kumasi, where, entirely through the continuing efforts of Arthur Morris over some seven years, the Burns Intensive Care Unit (BICU) was opened with due ceremony and the attendance of a number of local dignitories. The dedicated efforts of Mr Morris to build up the Reconstructive Plastic Surgery Unit and encourage the work of Dr Pius Agbenorku, the Reconstructive Plastic Surgeon in post – with the final formation of the BICU – was, as already mentioned, recognised by the university in Kumasi, by conferring on him a well-deserved Honorary Professorship.

The opening of the BICU in Kumasi, was the beginning of the fulfilment of what, in the early days, had been President Rawlings' vision of such Centres eventually being developed in all the main cities in Ghana – a wholly deserving cause which he never lost sight of, and constantly encouraged us to keep in mind despite the multitude of problems we had to deal with in Accra itself.

Now that I was really retired and had handed over the Chairmanship to Martyn, as Honorary President I could attend Committee Meetings, mostly held in Glasgow.

I was certainly going to miss my visits to Ghana, which had become part of my life for the past nine years, and in particular I was going to miss the small group of really close friends I had made: Eddie Yeboah, with whom I had shared from the beginning the development of this concept of giving Ghana a whole new caring branch of surgery; Bernard and Jennie Antoine, who had created a welcoming home for me when the earlier socialising of the first year or two had gradually dropped away; Evelyn Tay, who had done more than anyone to build up this service we had given to Ghana; Hein and Ellie Grüter, who had made me so welcome down at their beautiful, and restful, house at Big Ada, with the fishing trips which had been such a source of relaxation whenever I could manage to get away from the ever-present problems in Accra – and there was my eternal gratitude for Hein's design of the magnificent Centre, which draws praises from everyone who sees it. And I was certainly going to miss my very good friend Alex Kujiku, without whom I would never have seen so much of the beautiful countrysIde, or learned so much about the Ghanaian people.

One trip I had never made was to sail up the enormous lake that had formed when the Volta river was dammed at the narrows three miles downstream from Akosombo and when Alex suggested we might take a sail up the lake during what would probably be my last trip in Ghana, I just couldn't resist taking a day off my fairly crowded programme to see what some people regard as one of the most picturesque stretches of water anywhere in the world. The Volta lake, some two hundred and fifty miles in length and up to twenty miles wide in places, had five side prolongations, two on the west side, and three on the more populated east – up to forty miles long, and eight miles across in places. They had formed in the valleys where tributary rivers had run into the main Volta river before the waters rose, and helped to create a sheet of water almost a tenth the area of Ghana itself!

A quay had been built at Akosombo village, and small cargo vessels travelled from there all the way up to the small town of Kete Krachi, some one hundred and fifty miles from Akosombo, making stops at several of the villages along the eastern shore, most of which, with the border between Ghana and Togoland only some twenty miles to the east, formed Dr Alex Ababio's Parliamentary Constituency.

A mile round the shore from the cargo quay there was another small quay which served as a base from which several small passenger vessels made day or half-day trips up the lake, and Alex and I boarded one of these trim little vessels for a half-day trip.

The scenery on either side was magnificent, with the background of distant, and sometimes not so distant, hills on the west bank. We sailed up along the west bank, which had very few signs of habitation, and after a very adequate mid-morning snack in the dining cabin returned along the eastern shore, calling in at two of the small villages, with fishing boats hauled up on shore, where the usual display of carvings etc. was laid out to tempt the visitors.

It was a most enjoyable and relaxing experience, and a fitting way to bring down the curtain on my association with the Ghana I had come to know so well, and which I would rate as probably the most attractive of all the African countries I ever visited. To repeat what I have mentioned already, I have had the good fortune to visit some twenty African countries, one or two only briefly, but, because of the circumstances, most of them with plenty of opportunity to see something of the country itself – an opportunity which I always utilized whenever I got the chance – and as a result I was fortunate in really getting to know Africa better than most.

My fascination with this huge continent had actually had its beginnings in World War II, when, as an early volunteer surgeon in the Royal Army Medical Corps, I was posted to the British Military Hospital in Cairo – which gave me the opportunity on my leaves to explore every corner of Egypt, from the Valley of the Kings in the south to Alexandria and the whole extent of the northern coastline.

This idyllic existence was unfortunately abruptly terminated when, in June 1942, Rommel's army made its final push towards Egypt, and Cairo. Tobruk, the British Army's main supply port in Libya, due west of Egypt, became surrounded, and in the German bombardment that ensued one of the surgeons in the Military Hospital was killed. I was immediately shipped out as a replacement, from Alexandria, in a hospital ship which, although liable to be stopped and searched for arms and non-injured military, was still protected from capture under the Geneva Convention.

Tobruk eventually fell on 20 June, and we became Prisoners of War. Along with another doctor I made an unsuccessful attempt to escape, which did nothing to improve my relations with our captors, and I spent the next eighteen months in various places on the North African coast – admittedly not the best of circumstances to form an unbiased opinion about any country.

At the end of the war, however, when I had been invalided out of the army following a three-month stay in hospital, I was desperate to see the sun and feel the warmth of the tropics after a really bad winter in Scotland. After considering the options, I enlisted as a ship's Medical Officer in the Merchant Navy on board a cargo vessel, the *Clan Forbes*, which was about to make a four-month trip right round Africa, calling at every port of consequence to take on, or discharge, cargo.

The great advantage of being a ship's surgeon on a cargo ship, rather than on a luxurious passenger liner, is that when a ship goes into harbour the health care of the crew becomes the responsibility of the Harbour Medical Authority, and I was accordingly free to go ashore for the whole stay of the ship in harbour. On a passenger ship, on the other hand, the ship's medical officers are responsible for the health care of the passengers the whole time, in harbour or at sea.

This meant that I could travel reasonably widely in each place the ship was tied up in harbour, loading and unloading cargo – usually over four to five days – and I must have explored, even if briefly, almost every country right round the coast of Africa.

Of course, the Africa that I had had the good fortune to explore in those far off days had undergone great changes in the fifty years that had passed before the eventful occasion when the Argentine team had brought me to Ghana, where I ultimately became involved so intimately with the people of the country, and with their mode of life.

Whilst I had made many good friends in the course of the development of this new branch of surgery in Ghana, I also came to realise the innumerable problems that involvement in a venture such as we had undertaken would bring.

There were good moments and there were bad moments, and if the delays in the opening of the Nurses' Hostel had been something of a let down, the opening of Arthur's Burns Intensive Care Unit in Kumasi had helped diminish the disappointment.

When I flew back home on the 30th, my friend Rob Westerman, who had been invited to the Opening but could not attend, managed to squeeze me into the business class: so at least I had an undisturbed sleep. The association between the Project volunteers and KLM had started up in 1994 when I was canvassing the major airlines for donations, or for a free flight annually for one of the visiting surgeons. Lufthansa had only recently started up in Ghana, with a London-Accra flight via Frankfurt, and felt they could not help us meantime; Alitalia said no; Ghana Airways offered a reduced fare, but British Airways offered a better deal and we accepted this until some six months later, when I approached the then West African Manager of KLM, Mr Van Ess, who generously said KLM would donate four free flights a year for the volunteer surgeons coming out to Ghana. This totally unexpected gesture – one of the heaven-sent supportive actions which continues until the present day – meant that, apart from the four gifted flights, all our people travelled with KLM from then on. Without question the generous gesture of KLM was another of the major factors which helped to make the work of the Project succeed.

Reports, mainly through Mrs Tay, kept coming back to UK with what little could be found out regarding the progress of the quite extensive work that had to be carried out to install the water tanks, and typically the job seemed to be taking an extraordinary amount of precious time, during which the Hostel could not be used to start up the eagerly awaited advent of new nurses for the Centre. In the Centre itself the number of patients was inevitably continuing to creep up, and the shortage of nursing staff inevitably resulted in a limit to the actual surgery which could be carried out, and was putting a strain on everybody.

Nobody seemed to be able to find out what, if anything, was happening in the Hostel, and as the months dragged on with no indication of anything actually being done about the water tank problem, I had a sinking feeling that, for some reason or another, the apparent inaction was perhaps not happening by chance.

While all this was going on I got word that Monsieur Bernard Antoine was due to retire in October from his long-held position of manager of the Novotel Hotel. He and I had been close friends for almost seven years, and he was one of the most effective hotel managers I had ever known – always in evidence, speaking with hotel guests, it seemed all day – and over the years he had been of tremendous help to the Project, discounting hotel costs for visiting volunteer surgeons over the whole seven year period – and insisting I and Martyn were his personal guests. I was invited to attend a dinner which the hotel was giving in his honour, but I really felt that the journey to Ghana was getting a little bit beyond my capability.

And then I received a Fax from Bernard, saying that he and Jennie, his wife, would be greatly disappointed if I did not attend, and saying that he had specially invited the Japanese Ambassador, knowing how much we in the Project owed to the Japanese, and he thought that this would give me an opportunity to talk to the new Ambassador about the work we were doing in Ghana, and to thank him personally for all that they had done to help us. Bernard went on to say that Mr Westerman, who was also invited, had arranged that I should fly business class for a three-day trip without charge, and in the circumstances I felt I could scarcely turn all these good people down.

It was very enjoyable, of course, to meet old friends again, and Bernard had arranged that I would sit opposite himself, with the Japanese Ambassador, Mr Nitta, on one side of me, and his charming, petite wife on the other (the Ambassador was no great height himself). As Bernard had planned, I was able to thank the Ambassador for all that the Japanese people had done through the years to enable the Project to achieve what it had set out to do for Ghana. (They, and the British High Commission which, through the good offices of the successive High Commissioners, had, through the years, made numerous donations, and helped us replace worn-out equipment, were the only such bodies to help us.)

When I was called on to speak I was able to say as much to the whole gathering, and when I had finished, without waiting for anyone to call on him to respond, the Japanese Ambassador sprang to his feet and said that Japan was very impressed with what the Project had done, and he intended to continue to help with the donation of equipment for the Centre – which Martyn Webster told me some time later he had actually done – and promised to continue to assist the work we were carrying out in other ways in the future.

In the short time at my disposal – my hosts had arranged programmes visiting old friends – there was really no opportunity to learn anything definite about the Hostel problem. The frustration of not being able to get answers to my queries simply added to my feelings of gloom, and I began to wonder if the reality of the situation was that no one had the courage to tell me what the true situation was.

Although I received several invitations, I had no intention of going back to Ghana, and in view of the circumstances, Christmas was rather less merry than usual – at least for me – and hence I could scarcely believe it when, on 2 February 2002, I received a Fax from Fabian Mork telling me that the Hostel was finally opened, with the water supply flowing adequately on every floor! Most important of all was the follow-up news which we had all waited so long to hear, that the first new nurses had taken up residence, and were now working in the Centre: and that others were presently enquiring about coming to work there – with accommodation in the Hostel.

On 15 April 2002, Mr Webster, returning with Mr Arthur Morris from a very successful 2nd West African Course in Reconstructive Plastic Surgery and Burns, which again with the local help of Professor Yeboah and Mrs Tay, they had recently organised in Accra, reported that there were now 54 nurses on the Staff of the Reconstructive Plastic Surgery and Burns Centre, and that every bed and cot in the Centre was occupied!

CHAPTER 9

In the following two years, although not personally involved in the progress being made by Martyn and Arthur to continue their commitment to develop Ghana's ability to deal with the increasing volume of the sick and deformed who were, in many cases, travelling long distances seeking help, I was kept in the picture by letters from Evelyn Tay – and from the Board meetings that, as Honorary President, I was invited to attend.

It was encouraging to learn that great advances were being made to disseminate the knowledge of what could be done in the field of Reconstructive Plastic Surgery and Burns treatment by a series of Conferences in Accra to which not only Ghanaian practitioners, but surgeons from neighbouring countries, were invited to attend, and I will enlarge on this shortly.

Meantime, the situation in Ghana itself, with the increasing development of the Centre in Accra, and with the more recently formed BICU Centre in Kumasi growing apace, the surgeons were becoming more experienced and increasingly able to cope with some quite major surgical problems.

Fabian Mork (trained in Canniesburn) had reached retirement age, and Albert Paintsil (also trained in Canniesburn) had taken over as Head of the Centre. Fabian had continued to work on the staff of the Centre, partly on private cases and partly on non-private ones, to its great advantage. Two other younger surgeons, who had varying amounts of training in Cannisburn, had also joined the staff in junior capacities, and the volume of work being coped with in the Centre had reached a stage that would not hitherto have been thought possible.

Tony Laing, who had joined the staff of the Centre at its opening, and who was officially a lecturer on the University staff, had also reached retirement age; but like Fabian, he continued to work in the Centre as he had always done, partly involved with private patients, and partly seeing patients in the clinic.

One important step he had taken was to start up a clinic (outwith the scope of the Centre) in Cape Coast, the principal town on the wide sweep of the coastal region some 90 miles west of Accra. He visited Cape Coast Hospital once a month, saw patients in the clinic, and operated on the less complicated ones under local anaesthesia. The more complex patients were put on his list in the Centre in Accra.

This was a landmark in the history of Reconstructive Plastic Surgery in Ghana, for this was the first peripheral surgical clinic, unattached to a full-blown RPS Unit, that had been developed in Ghana – an action initiating what we hoped some day would take place widely throughout the country. As described earlier, the Reconstructive Plastic Surgery Unit in Komfo Anokje hospital in Kumasi had originally developed from single-day visits I had made there to see prospective patients every time I was in Ghana, starting from the time of the initial setting-up of the unit in Korle Bu Hospital in Accra in 1993, and later continued by visiting Volunteer Plastic Surgeons until 1995, when Arthur Morris took over going up to Kumasi as his sole objective during his visits – along with his nurse-trained wife Vicki – to what, with the existing posting there of Pius Agbenorku, had meant the establishment of a unit which could now cope with complicated, as well as routine, problems.

These visiting Volunteer Plastic Surgeons mentioned so often in this narrative came literally from all over the world, mostly from the UK, particularly Glasgow, but also from countries as far away as Australia. They came to help, in times of absence of Martyn and Arthur. (still working in the Health Service) with particularly complex problem cases, and many of them brought their own anaesthetist, since they had learned the hard way that obtaining an anaesthetist when required other than for a routine list (and even for those, at times) could prove a problem. Ghana owes a great deal to them, and their services over the years will always be valued.

Throughout the years Martyn and Arthur had organised, with the active local help of Prof. Yeboah and the indefatigable Mrs Tay, Instructional Courses, principally for Ghanaians but in fact embracing interested surgeons from all along the Gold Coast. At my request, Martin has contributed the following synopsis:

INSTRUCTIONAL COURSES IN GHANA
March 2000
>1st Pan-African Course on Reconstructive Plastic Surgery

March 2002
>2nd Pan-African Course on Reconstructive Plastic Surgery

Tutorials as well as lectures are also given when Visiting Surgeons come to Ghana
>e.g. *November 2003*
>>Care of patients undergoing treatment for cleft lip and palate
>>Acute reconstruction following trauma

>*January 2004*
>>Practical Course in Regional Anaesthesia for upper limb trauma

In addition, research into the distribution, causes and treatment of Buruli ulcer is being carried out in collaboration with the University of Glasgow, and a WHO. Grant has been applied for to support this work.

To return to the matter of Arthur's influence on the work in and around Kumasi: apart from the spreading of the surgical good news in the surrounding district, he was building up, along with Pius, an estimate of the possibilities of expanding into the country northwards and eastwards.

In the week before Christmas 2003, I received a letter from Evelyn Tay telling me, at the head of a number of other matters, that Arthur, along with his wife, had been up-country during their latest three-week stay in Ghana and had visited five northern cities with a view to finding out whether a Reconstructive Plastic Surgery and Burns centre might possibly be established there in due course!

As soon as it was possible, I got in touch with Arthur after his return in the first week in January 2004. He confirmed what Evelyn had written, but said it was six quite large cities, spread out widely in the northern country at distances from Kumasi varying from forty to a hundred and thirty miles.

It seems that, accompanied by his wife, he had on other occasions made extensive exploratory visits into the surrounding – and even more distant – areas, and particularly into the areas north of Kumasi, assessing the need for, and the possibility of developing, Reconstructive Plastic Surgery and Burns Units similar to the one in Kumasi. On this last visit he had identified six large towns (almost cities) where the facilities in the shape of good hospitals already existed, and in three of them it appeared that Pius had at one time or another carried out Reconstructive Plastic Surgery procedures although no special facilities for such surgery were yet in existence.

Arthur was kind enough to make a list of his comments with reference to each city, the region in which it is situated, and where specialised facilities might be developed:

1. Ashanti Region: Tontokrome. Tontokrome Health Centre – a nurse-led clinic in a Buruli ulcer area. No surgery. (unsuitable).
2. Agroyesum: St Margaret's Hospital, which has an excellent operating theatre. Some surgery performed there by Pius.
3. Kumasi: Nkawe-Toase Hospital. Small, but with a large number of patients with ulcers and chronic wounds. No surgery, but some minor surgery could be done.
4. Volta Region: Sogakope. Sogakope District Hospital. A new hospital with great potential for outreach care, including surgery.

5. Volta Region: Ketta. Ketta District Hospital. Potential for some outreach work if human resources allow.
6. Northern Region: Tamale. Tamale Teaching Hospital. This old building is about to undergo total refurbishment. There is a large need in this area for effective help. There is good road access, but travel time (6 hours) would stretch our resources beyond this limit at present.
7. Brong Ahafo Region: Sunyani Regional hospital. This is a superb brand new hospital built to replace several old ones. The enthusiastic management and staff give this Hospital the potential to provide a range of reconstructive surgery. Its possible attachment to the Medical School in Kumasi is an added bonus.

These visits, with the opportunity to see patients, operate and talk to staff have reinforced the view that the International Reconstructive Plastic Surgery Project is ideally placed to continue to spread its expertise to most, and hopefully all, regions of Ghana, given time. Unfortunately the chronic shortage of staff makes progress slow.

Apart from the above, one very special event during that December visit was a two-day Workshop on Wound Management, held in Komfo Anokji Hospital in Kumasi, and doctors and nurses from `All the regions of Ghana', to quote Arthur, were invited to attend.

Ninety-four participants were registered – although the head-count was always considerably higher, and `the Staff providing the teaching,' Arthur states, `were drawn from both Ghana itself, and also from a visiting group from Scotland of two senior nurses, two plastic surgeons, and an anaesthetist.'

This carrying of the good news widespread throughout the country – and the reaction of the Ghanaian People themselves – after the milestone visit of the Morrises, opened up a whole new vista for the Project; and with the excellent supervising of the functioning of the Centre in Accra by Martyn, who has toiled to such effect throughout the eleven years he has been my associate, the future looks really bright.

With this wonderful news, not only of the existing, but more importantly, of the certainty of the future spread of the Reconstructive Plastic Surgery facilities to which the Project was committed, I felt that the promise I had made some twelve years ago to President Rawlings that we would bring the benefits of Reconstructive Plastic Surgery and the treatment of burns to his country – all of it – was now on course to happen.

And only now could I accept the name the Ghanaians had given me so long ago.

OSEADAYO – `The one who keeps true to his word'.

Fig. 1: Clinic in Military Hospital, Accra: patient has severe facial scarring following burning incident. L–R Alberto Ferriols; Junior Argentine surgeon; anaesthetist

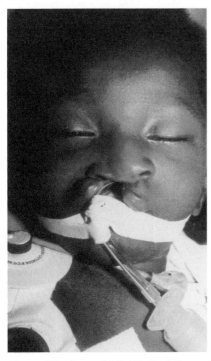 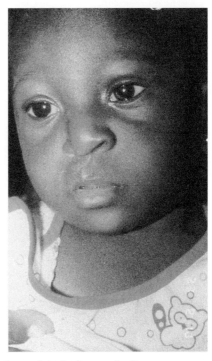

Above (fig. 2a and b): Cleft of lip and anterior palate before and after surgery

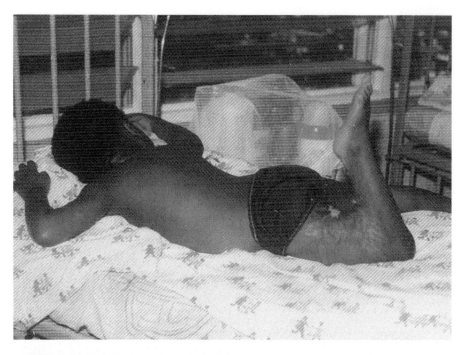

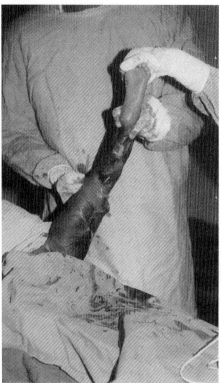

Fig 3a. Scarring of back of left leg following a severe burn two years before, in 5 year-old girl, holding the knee completely flexed.

Fig 3b. Surgery to the back of the leg to release scarring has resulted in complete freedom of movement of knee-joint

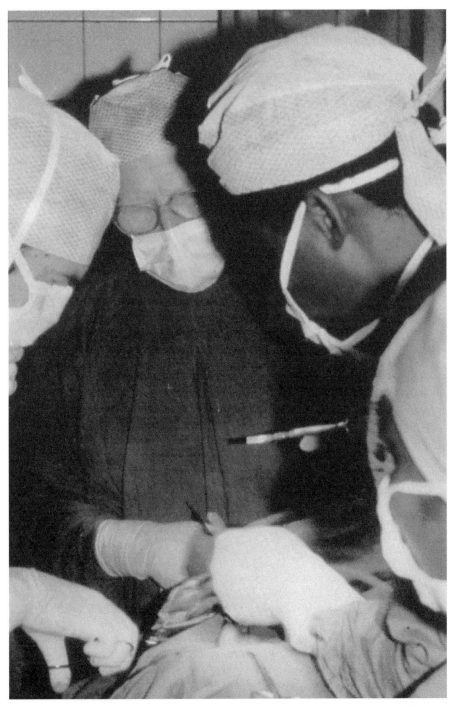

Fig 4: Mustardé operating: with Ferriols assisting on his right, and a Ghanian surgeon on his left

Fig 5: Speaking at the Accra Rotary Club, January 1993

Fig. 6: The first long-term volunteers in the Korle Bu unit – The Bainbridges,
January–June 1993 (On the Volta Water)

Fig. 7: Dr Alex Ababio, Deputy Minister of Health, joins the Bainbridge family, Prof. Yeboah and the author, as guests of President Rawlings at The Castle

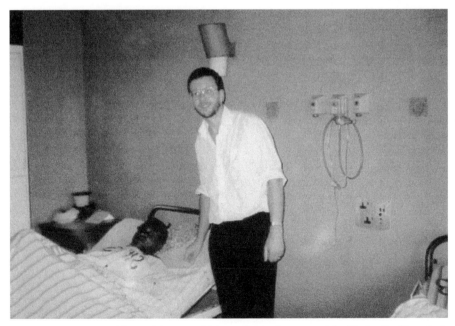

Fig. 8: Chris Bainbridge with one of his patients in a ward in Korle Bu Hospital

Fig. 9: The King of the Ashanti Nation greets Rex Cook and Prof. Mustardé in his palace in Kumasi

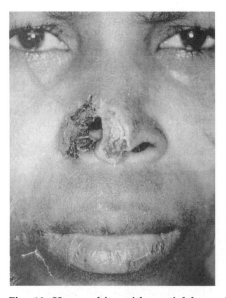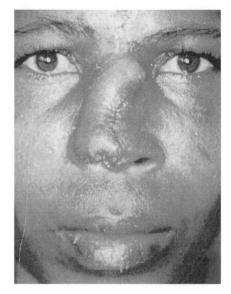

Fig. 10: Human bite with partial loss of nose. Treated by Mr Mork by bringing down a thick flap from the forehead. A complex manoeuvre carried out well

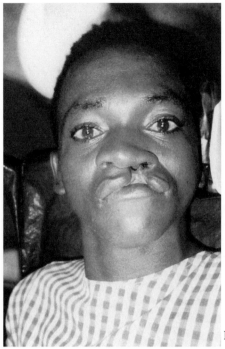

Fig. 11a: Before surgery

Fig. 11b: After surgery

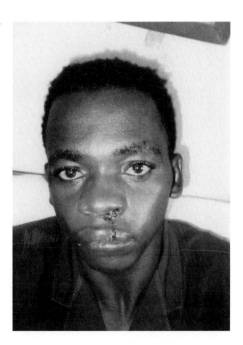

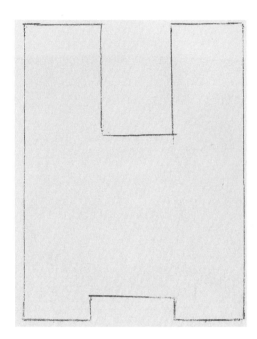

**Fig. 12: The elongated
'H' plan of Centre**

Fig. 13a: Front view of Reconstructive Plastic Surgery and Burns Centre (RPSBC)
     On opening Day – 27 May 1997

Fig. 13b: May 2002

Fig. 14a: Opening Day. Awaiting arrival of President Rawlings. Dias, with blue canopy, on left. Red and white canopy on right shelters VIPs.

Fig. 14b: Last minte discussions between Mrs Evelyn Tay and one of Protocol staff

Fig. 15a: Some of the Scottish Party patiently await the President's arrival. Front row, L–R, Mrs Maisie Mustardé, Mr David Mustardé, Mrs McDougle, Mr Rex Cook at the far end. Second row, Mr Martyn Webster, Mrs Shery Webster, Mrs Moureen Jones, Mrs Vicki Morris, Mr Arthur Morris

Fig. 15b: Medical staff, nurses, and friends, in the shade of the canopy facing dais

Fig. 16: Professor Mustardé welcomes the President

Fig. 17: Prof. Mustardé is honoured by being created an Officer of the Order of
the Volta, the highest honour that Ghana can confer on a non-Ghanian

Fig. 18: The cutting of the tape which the President invited Prof. Mustardé to carry out

Fig. 19: The President has a go with the pipes

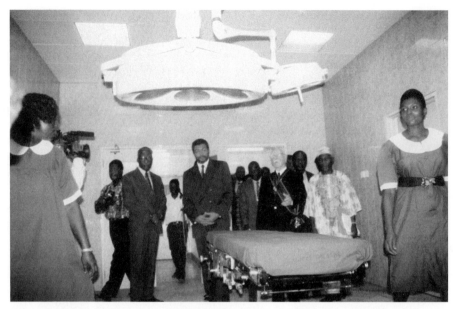

Fig. 20a and b: The President inspects the new operating theatre, and checks out the movement of the theatre light – as predicted he would do

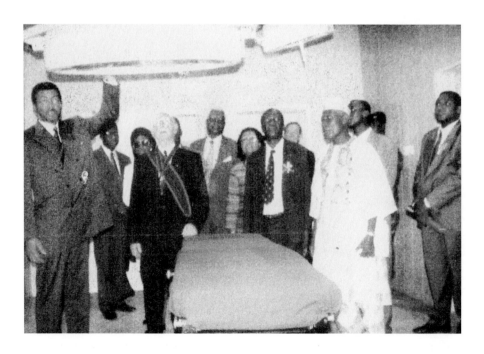

Fig. 21: The Paramount Chief, with his Court Officials – each carrying a staff headed by a solid gold emblem denoting his particular Court Office

Fig. 22: The Paramount Chief, accompanied by his senior wife, presents a mahogany carving to Prof. Mustardé, accompanied by his only wife

Fig. 23: Front hall of the Centre, looking towards the main wards, with the admission desk on the right, and the pharmacy on the left

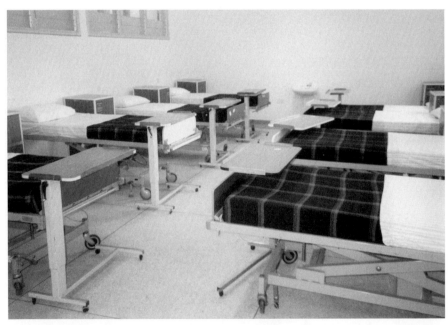

Fig. 24: One of the wards: equipped with beds, bedside tables and bedside cabinets, provided by The Ayrshire Hospital Trust, through the good offices of Mr Douglas Brown OBE, FRCS, at that time Chairman of the Board

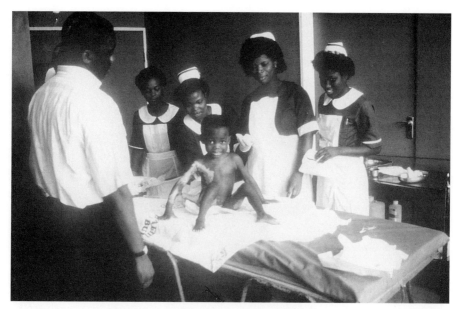

Fig. 25a: Severe burns treated in the Accident and Emergency Department

Fig. 25b: The Hostel for nurses working in the RPS & Burns Centre. This east-facing part of the building, with car park in front, bears the inscription JAPANESE BLOCK. The south-facing part of the building bears the inscription McNEE BLOCK

Fig. 26a: 'So you are the man who causes all the trouble!'

Fig. 26b: 'But I get things done, Ma'am...'

Fig. 27a: The Princess is given a guided tour

Fig. 27b: "Goodbye – and Good Luck"

Fig. 28a: The Burns Intensive Care Unit (BICU), Komfo Anokye Teaching Hospital, Kumasi. Making the final preparations for opening.
L–R Mr Arthur Morris – volunteer, Nana Otuo Serebu – Chairman Hospital Board; Mrs Vicki Morris – nurse and wife of volunteer

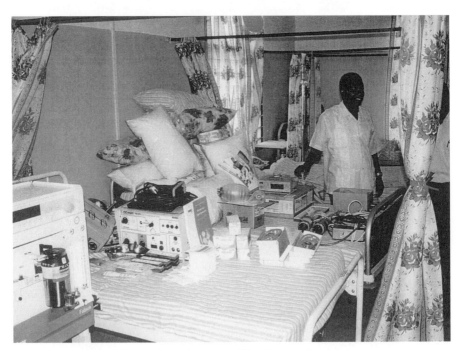

Fig. 28b: A mass of donated equipment still to be put in place

Fig. 29: Opening ceremony, 1 February 2001

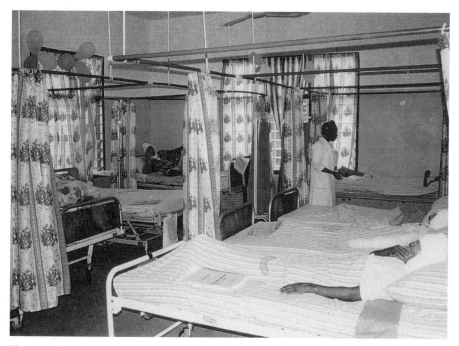

Fig. 30: The beds begin to fill up

Fig. 31a: Fishermen's village

Fig. 31b: Setting up a fire to smoke the fish their husbands have caught

Fig. 32: Children's Block (white building is operating theatre suites)

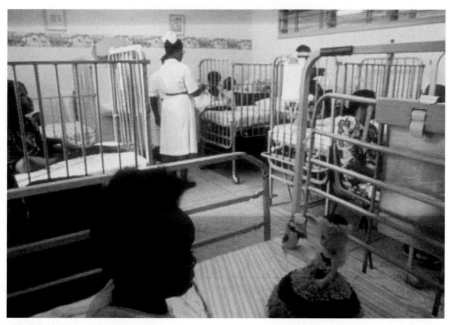

Fig. 33: Infant's ward in the Centre. Cots donated by the Royal Hospital for Sick
Children, Yorkhill, Glasgow

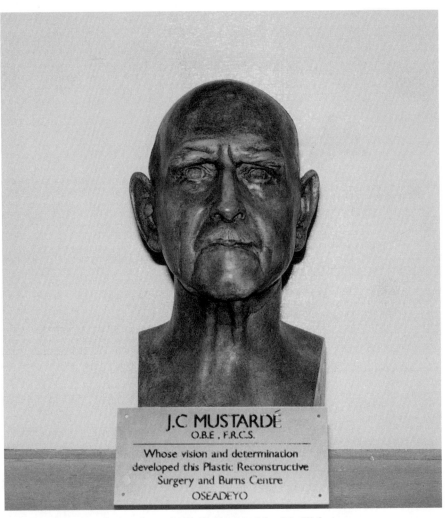

Fig. 35: Bronze sculpture in main hall. Donated by Mr Webster

All Profits from the book will go to the Ghana Project.